ASPEN PUBLISHERS

A PRACTICAL GUIDE TO APPELLATE ADVOCACY
Third Edition

Teacher's Manual

MARY BETH BEAZLEY
Associate Professor of Law
Moritz College of Law
The Ohio State University

Wolters Kluwer
Law & Business

AUSTIN   BOSTON   CHICAGO   NEW YORK   THE NETHERLANDS

www.AspenLaw.com

ISBN 978-07355-8511-9

Aspen Publishers
Attn: Permissions Department
76 Ninth Avenue, 7th Floor
New York, NY 10011-5201

Copies of this Manual and the associated PowerPoint slides are available in electronic form. Teachers who have adopted the textbook may obtain a copy of the files, free of charge, by calling an Aspen Publishers sales assistant at 1-800-950-5259, or by emailing lgaledu@wolterskluwer.com.

Table of Contents

Changes from Second Edition to Third Edition

In Chapter 1, a brief discussion of writing theory has been added, focusing on the cognitivist and social perspective. In Chapter 2, relevant citations have been updated. In particular, the discussion of the standard of review for a motion to dismiss has been expanded. In particular, the recent cases from the United States Supreme Court (Twombly and Iqbal) are cited. Also, the text notes that some courts use the terms "pleading standard" and "legal standard" instead of the phrase "standard of review." The discussion of summary judgment motions is also slightly expanded.

In Chapter 3, the term "super search terms" has been changed to "foundational search terms." The text includes an expanded discussion of how to harvest arguments, and both good and bad examples of harvesting an argument. The chapter also includes a reference to some of the difficulties students may have when transferring from Google to other search methods. Chapter 4 includes no significant changes.

Chapter 5 includes two significant changes. First, it includes a discussion of when *not* to use the CREXAC formula, and introduces four labels to use to describe the ways in which a writer can report the result of the analysis of a legal issue: (1) Ignore, (2) Tell (one-sentence statement), (3) Clarify (CRAC analysis), and (4) Prove (CREXAC analysis). Further, Chapter 5 now includes a section on dealing with the opponent's arguments. This section is an expanded discussion of the section on dealing with an opponent's *authorities* that was included in chapter 6 in previous editions. This section discusses Professor Kathryn Stanchi's scholarship on this issue. It also notes that the locus of the controversy may dictate where it is discussed. For example, if the parties disagree on what the rule is, the writer will address the opponent's argument differently than if they disagree on how the rule applies.

In Chapter 6, as noted above, the discussion of how to address an opponent's authorities has been moved to Chapter 5 (and expanded). Accordingly, teachers should note that the subsections within Chapter 6 will have different enumeration than in past editions. Chapter 6 also includes a new sub-section within the section on case descriptions: Accuracy in Case Descriptions. This section gives advice on how to avoid common problems in mischaracterizing cases. The section on Tom Brokaw Introductions has been changed to Katie Couric Introductions. The section on unpublished decisions has been updated and notes that these decisions are often referred to as "nonprecedential" decisions

Chapter 7 includes no major changes. In Chapter 8 the formal requirements for appellate briefs and formal requirements for motion briefs are presented in two separate sections. Although this change has resulted in some repetition, the change allows teachers to assign students to read either Section 8.4 *or* Section 8.5 to learn relevant formal requirements. The text brings in more examples of local rules and discusses courtesy copies and electronic filing in a bit more detail.

Chapter 9 illustrates how to incorporate language from a pleading standard for a motion into a question presented. In the section on the statement of facts, the chapter introduces concepts of narrative reasoning and storytelling theory, citing some of the relevant scholarship on this matter. Chapter 10 expands the discussion of Topic Sentences to focus on how to use topic sentences in the explanation section as a method to lay a foundation for analogizing or distinguishing authority cases. The "roadmap" section of the chapter introduces the concept of "legal backstory" to describe the information that should appear in introductory material that precedes the roadmap.

There are no major changes in Chapter 11. Chapter 12 added another method for easing proofreading on the computer: Enlarging text to a larger font. Teachers should be sure that students understand that this method is to use only when proofreading and that font must be returned to normal size before filing the document. Chapter 13 gives advice on keeping a poker face when arguing, and gives more specific advice on what to do when asked a question that you don't understand. Chapter 14 includes no major changes.

Appendix A includes no major changes. Appendix B has eliminated the specific text of court rules (which may be out of date). Instead, it lists relevant websites for court rules and gives general advice for finding court rules as well as local rules and standing orders. Appendix C is largely unchanged, although it changed a party name in the sample motion brief: Burton Cork, Inc. was changed to to Marvin-Kobacker, Inc.

Teacher's Manual

Preface and Presumptions

This textbook presumes that students using it will be working on either an appellate brief or a motion brief during the course of the semester. This teacher's manual contains ideas for lectures, in-class discussions, in-class demonstrations, and in and out-of-class exercises. The Professor Materials on the book's website at http://www.aspenlawschool.com/books/appellate_advocacy/ contain the entire text of this teacher's manual (as well as color versions of some material not amenable to text format) so that the teachers who have adopted the text can easily create handouts. You may wish to look at the materials on the website while you review the teacher's manual so that you can look at certain handouts (e.g., the sample syllabus, the sample criteria sheets) while you are reading about them. In addition to the material noted above, the website also contains PowerPoint presentations tied to the text.

To access the Professor Materials on the website, you will need to obtain a password by calling an Aspen Publishers sales assistant at 1-800-950-5259 or by emailing legaledu@wolterskluwer.com.

This teacher's manual will give ideas for exercises that can use textbook-based materials (such as the sample briefs), but it will also recommend exercises based on the case the students are working on. For some chapters, you may wish to do both a textbook-based exercise and a case-based exercise, to contrast the different results with each; for others, you may wish to do only one type of exercise, or neither exercise.

The need for or usefulness of in-class exercises varies depending on the size of the class, the particular dynamics of the class, the number of classroom hours available, whether the class meets for a 50-minute session or for a longer session, and on many other variables. Therefore, I do not presume that every teacher who uses this textbook will complete every exercise, or even any of them. The exercises are provided as a tool to help to enhance the learning experience, to reinforce certain principles, or to communicate ideas more effectively to various students in the classroom by communicating them in a different way.

Some exercises can be completed in small groups or with the whole class during class time, while others may be more effective if the students do some work on their own either before or after the class meeting. **Therefore, when planning a particular class meeting, you may want to look ahead to the teacher's manual guidance on upcoming chapters to see if you want to give the students an out-of-class assignment to provide a foundation for in-class work for the next week's class.**

This textbook also presumes that this course is *not* the students' introduction to legal research and legal writing, even though it may be the teacher's first time teaching a writing course (the first course I ever taught on my own was appellate advocacy). Thus, this teacher's manual will not devote significant time to a general discussion of how to teach legal writing, although I will address teaching methods that I believe can be used effectively in conjunction with the assignments and exercises that the textbook contemplates. For general advice about teaching legal writing, I recommend reviewing the texts and teacher's manuals of any or all of the following excellent books: Linda H. Edwards, <u>Legal Writing: Process, Analysis, and Organization</u> (Aspen 5th ed. 2010); Richard K. Neumann, Jr., <u>Legal Reasoning and Legal Writing</u> (Aspen 6th ed. 2009); or Laurel Currie Oates, Anne M. Enquist, and Kelly Kunsch, <u>The Legal Writing Handbook</u> (Aspen 5th ed. 2010).

Finally and perhaps most importantly, this textbook presumes that the teacher will be using a writing-process approach, by which I mean that the teacher will intervene in and conduct some sort of review of the students' work before the final draft is completed. Scholars have divided (or, more appropriately, arranged) the writing process into both a variety of pieces and a variety of Venn diagrams. I think in terms of prewriting (including research planning, research, and writing planning), writing and revising (including creating a first draft and revising for substance and organization), and polishing (including sentence-level editing and proofreading). The sample syllabus contemplates three drafts. First, the students are asked to complete a "macro draft," which consists of only the argument section. The purpose of this draft is to focus the student's attention on issues of content, large-scale organization, and legal analysis.

The second draft, or "micro draft," consists of the entire document, from the cover page to the certificates of service and compliance. In this draft, the student's focus broadens to include issues of persuasion and audience, as well as small-scale format concerns that are important in any document presented to a court. The third and final draft, cleverly called "the final draft," is identical to the micro draft, except in how it is graded. This teacher's manual (and the accompanying website) will contain sample criteria sheets that can be used for outlines or drafts at various stages of the process; the philosophy behind the critiquing method is explained below.

Because this second edition of the text has been expanded to include motion briefs, the teacher's manual also includes samples of criteria sheets for motion briefs. You may need to alter these criteria sheets, depending on your own course requirements. For example, because many motion briefs do not require a table of contents, table of authorities, summary of argument, etc., these elements are not listed. You may decide to require that students include these elements in a motion brief; you can find references to them in the sample criteria sheets for the appellate briefs.

Designing the Syllabus:

A sample syllabus is reprinted below, and you may wish to copy it exactly. However, before you adopt or create a syllabus, you must keep several things in mind. First, you must know your level of certainty as to how the semester will progress. Second, you must decide what types of work product you will require students to turn in to you over the course of the semester. Finally, you must decide on realistic due dates, conference dates, and oral argument dates.

2

When deciding what types of work product you will require from the students, consider your workload and the students' workload as well as the pedagogical benefits of any assignments. In general, I restrict my out-of-class assignments to assignments directly related to the current project. In other words, I am merely requesting that the students turn in work that they should be doing on their own in order to create a good final draft by the due date. (This is not to say that it is always wrong to assign homework not based on the students' case; if the case is straightforward, if it will not teach certain essentials, or if the course's credit hours are higher than average, outside assignments may well be appropriate.)

For example, you could ask students to turn in a research plan, a research journal showing the results of the research, an outline, an annotated outline, and three or more drafts of the brief itself. Most teachers do not have time to critique or even review all of these assignments. Of course, you should not presume that assignments are not helpful unless they can be critiqued individually. In a small-section course, I have often required students to turn in all of the items on the list above, but I have provided individual critique only on two or three of them. For the others, I reviewed all of the work turned in – or enough of it to give me an idea of the class's general understanding – and used that knowledge to inform what we did in class.

When deciding what to make students turn in for your review or critique, you might choose those assignments that have pedagogical benefits that cannot be replicated through reading or in-class work *and* that are reasonable given the time and credit limitations imposed on you and your students.

Once you have tentatively decided on the types of assignments you will assign, you can schedule your semester. I say "tentatively" on purpose. Like the writing process, designing a syllabus can be a recursive process, and time considerations may cause you to reconsider earlier plans. Any legal writing course must take logistics into account, including the time you will need to critique and return papers, the time students will need to review your critique before any conferences, and the time needed for the students to revise the papers before the next due date. An appellate advocacy course must usually consider time for oral arguments and ideally for practice arguments. I find that the best way for me to design my syllabus is to use my word-processing program to generate and print a calendar for the relevant months. Then I can physically see the days that I have allotted for brief-grading, for conferences, for revision, and for practice and performance arguments.

It is important to give students sufficient time to revise after receiving your written critique or meeting with you in conference. If you have a high number of students, it may not be realistic to hand back all papers on the same day; during a year in which I taught 72 students, I had rolling due dates: the revision was due one week after the student met with me in conference, and the students knew that they could expect their papers in their student mailboxes two days before the conference was scheduled. In this way, instead of having one deadline for returning 72 papers, I had six deadlines of 12 papers each. (Frankly, it was horrible no matter how you sliced it, but the rolling due dates made my life a little easier and eliminated student complaints of unfairness.)

When scheduling reading assignments and due dates for written assignments, make sure that the reading assignments provide guidance on the types of work product you are asking for. For example, you should generally not require students to write a complete draft before you have discussed how to write a statement of facts.

With a couple of exceptions, the book can be assigned in order. The chapters on oral argument appear at the end of the book, but some teachers may want to have the students conduct practice arguments before the final draft is finished (in fact, I recommend this method), and so should assign oral argument readings earlier. Further, Chapter 11 covers persuasive writing techniques, but because these techniques permeate the document, and even the writing process, some teachers may want to assign this chapter early in the semester and then come back to it as needed later on.

I have included most of the "front matter" of policies and procedures within the sample syllabus because it may be helpful to teachers who have never designed a syllabus before. I spell out honor code and late paper requirements in the syllabus because I find that doing so prevents some problems and creates an easy reference point for problems that may occur down the road. I have included two sample schedules; one that contemplates ten weeks of meetings, and one that contemplates fourteen weeks of meetings. If your class meets more than once per week, you may wish to divide the readings accordingly; on the other hand, you may wish to have the entire assignment read before the first meeting of the week so that you can use all class hours for discussion or exercises related to the entire reading assignment.

I have found that students are sometimes reluctant to do the reading in a legal writing course, perhaps because most legal writing courses do not include a final exam. You may wish to pique their interest in the readings by including a teaser, either orally or in writing, about the next class. For example, the first chapter includes a discussion about how the fable of the sun and the wind relates to legal writing. When you post your assignment you could add the note, "In the first class meeting we will discuss course requirements, due dates, and what it means for an appellate advocate to 'be the sun.'" This method has some risks (some students are turned off by anything they consider to be "cutesy," while others may skim the readings, looking *only* for the information relevant to the teaser), but you may decide that the risks are worth the possible increase in the number of students who complete the readings. I find that if I can get students to do *any* reading, they will discover that class does not duplicate the readings, and so they are inclined to read more. Of course, I have tried to write the book in such a way that the students will find that it helps them to write more easily and effectively, and thus, I hope that they will want to do the readings. I have included at least one possible teaser with each chapter description below; each is followed by the section in the book where you can find the information about the teaser (of course, I recommend NOT sharing that with the students!).

Using Student Work in Class:

A large screen in the classroom is an important tool for any legal writing teacher. Whether you use an overhead projector, a laptop, or a document camera (formerly known as "an opaque projector"), the ability to have the entire class looking at work on a large screen can help explore and explain many concepts. With a screen, a teacher can write and revise with a laptop, can put student work up on an overhead or document camera, or can have students point out strengths and weaknesses in various writing samples. Throughout this teacher's manual, I have used the word "overhead" to refer both to materials created to show to the whole class, or to a machine (whether an LCD projector, an overhead projector, or a document camera) used to show them to the class (e.g., "You can put an overhead of student work on the overhead to make this point"). Perhaps obviously, document cameras and LCD projectors work even better than an overhead projector that uses transparencies; thus, if you have not yet made the transition from the traditional overhead, I recommend that you do so if you get the chance.

The text contains four sample briefs (three appellate briefs and one motion brief) that can be used as fodder for discussion. I often find, however, that the most effective discussions are discussions of the case that the students are currently working on. In-class group work can accomplish this goal effectively, if group work is feasible (i.e., the room is well-designed for group work, you have enough class time to allow the students to complete the task *and* share the product of their work with the class, and the number of students is manageable).

Sophie Sparrow, of the Franklin Pierce Law Center, has advocated requiring written class preparation to promote effective group work. For some in-class exercises, she refuses to allow students into class if they have not completed the preparation (which is usually a quite short and simple written task). I have had great success using this method, and I recommend it. If you are not comfortable with the idea of turning students away, you might be able to achieve much of the same effect by having the students complete the written preparation before the in-class group work begins. For example, you could have students read the record and complete a list of three ideas for beginning research, three facts that are good for the petitioner, and three facts that are good for the respondent. In the alternative, you could assign only the reading and have students complete the three lists in class as a prelude to the group work. Although I recommend the first alternative, I think that group work is almost always more effective if the participants begin with some sort of written preparation.

If group work is not feasible (or as an alternative to group work), you may wish to require students to turn in small homework assignments the day before the class meeting. When I use this method, I do not return these assignments or give any sort of grade; the student merely receives a check mark for having fulfilled the requirement. However, by quickly reviewing what the students turn in, I get a good idea of how well they understood the readings, and I have a basis for class discussion. If you ask students to e-mail the assignment to you, you can easily block and copy (and perhaps edit) representative samples of work and create transparencies to use on an overhead projector, or project them via laptop or document camera. I prefer that the students send me these assignments within the e-mail message rather than as an attachment. I use Wordperfect software, which allows me to remove codes and change fonts, etc. easily, and I prefer not to have to open 50 or 60 separate attachments (as happens with my large-enrollment appellate advocacy course). In the alternative, you can have the students use a digital drop box in a Lexis or Westlaw webcourse.

When I use student work in class, I observe a couple of ground rules. First, all student work is anonymous. Second, I use examples that are either good examples or *classic* mistakes – i.e., mistakes that lots of people made (or mistakes that I recognize as being common, even if only one person turned in a document with that mistake). That is, I don't put up the horrendously bad, once-in-a-lifetime-unbelievable mistakes. I tell the students my ground rules before I ever put student work up on the overheads. I teasingly warn them that they shouldn't shout "hey, that's mine!" until they know whether it's a good or bad example, but that if it's a bad example, they know they have company. If a student used a unique word or phrase, I may edit some part of the example so that the student will not be 100% sure who the bad example belongs to.

Although I never put work up on the overhead to make fun of it, some mistakes are naturally funny. If some people burst into spontaneous laughter at a bad example, I immediately take care to assign the mistake to as large a group as possible, e.g., "do you *know* how many of the petitioners turned in something like this?" In this way, no one student has to feel bad about the mistake, but all can learn from it. I want them to be able to laugh at their mistakes, and not to take them so seriously. If they are able to laugh at themselves, they're able to really see what they've written, and that makes it more likely that they can edit effectively.

Using Criteria Sheets

This teacher's manual includes criteria sheets for an annotated outline, a macro draft, a micro draft, and a final draft for an appellate brief, and for a motion brief. Some teachers may not require students to turn in each of these assignments; in my course, students do not turn in an annotated outline, for example. You will note that only the final draft includes a place for a teacher to write a real score; on the others, teachers give a "minus zero" to a brief that meets the requirements adequately, and deducts points (that will later be deducted from the score on the final draft) from briefs that fail to meet the requirements. Teachers may also give a dicta grade on the micro draft.

Obviously, you may decide to use, adapt, or ignore the enclosed criteria sheets. It may help you to know the reasoning behind some of the features they include. The purpose of avoiding a "real" score until the final draft is to encourage students to work hard on early drafts without undue penalties. I believe that this method promotes realistic practice in using the writing process. For example, when I write, I may not edit for punctuation problems and citation form until the very end, so I do not penalize students for these problems until the final draft. Some have questioned having penalties at all on the early drafts, but I have found the penalties necessary for three reasons: 1) Law students are the kings and queens of the cost-benefit analysis, and unless there is a strong possibility of a penalty, they won't work hard on early drafts. 2) We are paid to read and critique early drafts. If students turn in less than a good faith effort, we are wasting time (and thus, money) critiquing work that the student could improve without our help. 3) Even without penalties, students who do a bad job on the first draft rarely do a great job on the final draft. By encouraging good work on the first draft, we increase the chances for a good final draft.

In my course, I require one partial draft and two full drafts. On the two pre-final drafts, the maximum score is 0 points (the best they can get is "minus zero"). If the student has made a good faith effort to meet the criteria, he or she earns a "minus zero." If, however, there has been a significant misunderstanding of the problem, or a noticeable lack of effort or work, I may deduct up to 15 points. Any points deducted from the first two drafts will be deducted from the student's raw score on the final draft, which is on a 65-point scale (I purposely use an uneven number because it is harder for the students to convert the raw score to a "grade") .

IMPORTANT: *Rarely, if ever,* will all 15 points be deducted. I made the number that high to threaten the students into performing (it usually works, too). For an outrageous problem (e.g., the student turned in a list of cases or an unsupported outline for a draft), I might deduct 10-15 points. For significant offenses (a student ignored an important issue, missed more than one important authority, etc.), a 2-3 point deduction might be appropriate. For minor problems, a one point deduction usually gets the message across.

I frequently deduct 0 points from the drafts because the students do work hard on the drafts. My goal is to be consistent. Because the points off come off the final score, I find that taking off too many points on early drafts can discourage the students from working hard on later drafts – if they're starting out with a 55, they may think, why should they bother? However, if a student has significantly failed the first draft, AND if I have the time to do it for all students in this situation (rarely more than one), I may take off a high number of points but allow the student to submit an interim draft to "earn back" some – but not all – of the lost points. I impose strict controls on the students in a situation like this.

Each criteria sheet is keyed to the type of draft demanded. The first draft (as opposed to an outline) is the MACRO draft, and its focus is mainly content and large-scale organization. The second draft is the MICRO draft, and its focus broadens to include small-scale organization and signals to the reader. The focus of the FINAL draft is broadest, and it includes grammar and mechanics. All of the criteria sheets encourage comments on all of these areas, but points are deducted only for failing to meet the enumerated criteria.

Each criteria sheet asks questions keyed to the various requirements (for example, "did the writer focus each section of the document on one issue or sub-issue?"). Whenever possible, I answer the questions noted on the criteria sheet (e.g., "yes," "no," "sometimes," "rarely," "usually," etc.). The students can then use the criteria sheet to help them know what areas need more work than others. I also use the final comment section of the criteria sheet for this purpose. In the final comment, I provide space to comment on four areas ("Content and Large-scale Organization," "Legal Analysis," "Writing Style," "Mechanics"). Because I usually type my comments, I don't need to leave myself much space for the final comment; I use the final comment space to refer the students to my typed final comment, in which I use these same head-ings. If you hand-write your comments, you may wish to give yourself more space for the final comment.

The Final Comment space on the criteria sheet also contains a space in which I can check the suggested level of revision needed for each of the four elements. I added this feature because it is impossible for any writing teacher to find and mark every possible problem on a draft. Unfortunately, some students get the impression that all they have to do is fix the marked sentences and make an attempt to address the specific issues raised. By checking the suggested level of revision, I can give the students an overall impression of how much work remains and, hopefully, keep the responsibility with them. Each element has four categories, and three of the four categories have two sub-categories. The teacher can check "significant revision needed," "moderate revision needed," "minimal revision needed," or "don't touch it." For the first three categories, the teacher can also check either "throughout," or "as noted" for each.

No matter how much detail I have provided as to a particular aspect of the brief, either in marginal comments or the final comment, I make sure to state or check the amount of revision needed for each element. I never check "Don't touch it," because they won't. I try to err on the side of encouraging more work. On the other hand, I try not to check "significant revision needed throughout" for all four elements unless it is absolutely necessary, because I think it would be too discouraging. I will often check for various elements "significant revision needed as noted, moderate revision throughout." This comment is appropriate if the student has a few significant problems in an area (that my comments point out), while the rest of the document is adequate but would benefit from more work.

In addition to providing a space for taking points off, the criteria sheet also allows me to provide a "Dicta Grade" on the Micro Draft (I have sometimes given a dicta grade on the Macro Draft as well). I added this element to the criteria sheets because in the past, some students who earned a minus 0 on the first two drafts thought that they had a perfect paper, when I had been trying to signal that they had been working hard and meeting minimal requirements. These students would do almost no revision, or would change only the specific items I had marked, and then react with astonishment to any grade lower than 100%. (The "revision needed" categories discussed above are also geared toward this problem.)

The dicta grade does *not* indicate the potential grade of a future draft if suggested work is accomplished. The dicta grade *does* indicate my gut reaction as to what grade that draft would receive if it were a final draft. *It is vitally important to low-ball dicta grades. Some students (whose futures lie in litigation, after all) take the dicta grade as a promise of a "floor" below which their grade cannot sink.*

I find that it is better to err on the C side of the curve rather than the A side. A dicta grade of C- is a great motivator for many students; my policy is that I never give a paper higher than a C+ for a dicta grade. I sometimes warn students of the lack of value of the dicta grade. The only message for most of them is that they still have work to do. I warn students who have "high" dicta grades not to rest on their laurels; a paper that is currently the best may end up near the bottom after everyone else pours the work on for the next draft. If I think a student is in danger of a D or an F, I may leave the dicta grade blank, and fill it in during the conference. It is important to let them know if they are in danger of a D or an F, but receiving a paper with a D or an F on it, even though it is "dicta," can be traumatic.

If I decide to put the dicta grade on the paper, and I think it should be lower than a C-, I usually add some sort of explanatory comment that I put right next to the dicta grade, e.g., "because of misunderstanding re: issues" or whatever. I do not try to curve the dicta grades; they frequently are all C's, or range from C+ to C-. I don't work that hard on choosing perfect dicta grades because the precedential value of dicta – none – is the same as the grade value of the dicta grade. One of the reasons I use the grading system that I use is that I want my time and energy at this stage to go into the critique rather than into calibrating grades.

Occasionally, a student will complain that he or she received a final grade lower than the dicta grade. My first question to them is "what's the precedential value of dicta?" When they reply "nothing," I say, "that's the value of the dicta grade. The real grade is what counts, and I hope that no students base their work decisions on their dicta grades rather than on the comments and answers to the criteria sheet questions." Of course, the better solution is to avoid having to make this explanation: lowball the dicta grades so that it is essentially impossible for a student to receive a final grade that is lower than the dicta grade.

Critiquing and Conferencing Advice

You may wish to consult the books and teacher's manuals referenced above for detailed advice on critiquing and conferencing, but I will provide a few ideas on how to critique drafts of briefs. I believe that conferences can be a particularly effective teaching tool in legal writing. The best way to make conferences effective is to provide a sufficiently detailed critique, to have some sort of an agenda for each conference, and to give the students time to review your critique before the conference. For more information on critiquing and conferencing, you may also wish to consult Mary Kate Kearney and Mary Beth Beazley, *Teaching Students How to "Think Like Lawyers": Integrating Socratic Method With the Writing Process*, 64 Temple L. Rev. 885 (1991).

From a mechanical viewpoint, I believe that a thorough critique is easier to complete in typewritten form. Instead of writing marginal notes on the paper, I write a number in the margin, and then type a comment that corresponds to that number. Students read the paper and the typed comments side-by-side. This method gives the paper a neater appearance (students no longer accuse me of "bleeding" all over their papers) and allows me to use and/or adapt pre-fabricated comments over and over again for common problems. Many legal writing faculty now use computer programs to "embed" their comments. Programs that put the comments in the margins have the same benefits – and perhaps more – than typewritten comments on a separate paper. Because I use WordPerfect macros, and those cannot yet be used on my system, I still type my comments separately. I will note, however, that many of my colleagues who critique electronically still find it beneficial to have a hard copy of the student paper in front of them while they critique. The ability to flip forward and back and to see whole paragraphs and whole pages at a glance can be particularly important to an effective critique.

1.   **Preparing to critique**

Before beginning, read over any materials you have on the assignment (e.g., facts, cases, statutes, briefs, outlines). Highlight citations and important facts and analysis in your materials to make things easier for you to find. Make sure that you have the text and a good dictionary handy. You may wish to scan through a few papers without marking them so that you have some idea of how the group did the assignment. Note that marking in pencil lets you change your mind.

Generally, I assign half of my students to each side of the case, and so my first step is to separate the papers into petitioner and respondent stacks. Next, I stack them from the longest paper to the shortest paper within each stack. This is based on advice from my sister, Trish Sanders, who was a veteran teacher of freshman composition. Generally, the best papers are found among the longest ones, and the weakest among the shortest ones. By critiquing from best to worst, generally speaking, you will learn what students were capable of doing with the assignment, and you will be better prepared to tackle the weaker papers. For myself, I find that it is a bad idea to start with the weaker papers. I spend too much time agonizing over the comments and wondering if my expectations were too high. If, on the other hand, I read the weaker papers at the end of a critiquing session, I am better informed. If 7 of the 8 students assigned to that side of the case have found a particular argument, I know that I am not being too demanding to expect to see it in the brief.

2.   **Commenting on the paper**

Decide how to prioritize your comments. Generally, in early drafts, your first priority should be to identify content and organizational problems. Except when correcting a final draft, try to save comments on style and mechanics for your final comment, and use that comment to note the *type* of mistake that the student seems to make, rather than correcting each of the student's errors. Often, "writing" errors lessen or disappear once the student figures out exactly what he or she intended to say and discovers a valid organizing principle, and so it wastes both your time and the students' time to correct small-scale errors at an early stage.

Unless you tell them otherwise, students will presume that all comments have equal weight. Thus, I label each of my numbered comments as "A," "B," or "C" comments. I tell the students that when they are revising, they should make revisions related to "A" comments first because these comments address content, large-scale organization, and other important issues. They should then make revisions related to "B" comments; these comments address small-scale organization, writing style, and other medium-level concerns. Finally, they should make revisions related to "C" comments, which address mechanics and other minutiae. I make this suggestion because a "C" comment on a sentence (e.g., pointing out a punctuation error) does not necessarily mean that I expect that particular word, phrase, sentence, or paragraph to appear in the next draft. It just means that I want to make the student aware of that error. If they revise in A, B, and C order, they may find that other guidance (e.g., "improve your analysis of X issue") makes them eliminate or drastically revise certain sections of the document When they get to that C comment, they may find that they have already decided to eliminate the sentence. The comment can still be valuable, however, for its illustration of and guidance about a particular type of error. All of my typed comments open with a paragraph that goes something like this:

> Comments are designated as "A" comments, "B" comments, or "C" comments. When revising, please consult "A" comments first: they are focused on significant issues like content and large-scale organization. Consult "B" comments second: they are focused on mid-level issues like writing style and signals to the reader. Consult "C" comments last: they are focused on less significant issues like punctuation and citation form. Particularly with C comments, realize that sentence with a comment may need to be eliminated for the next draft. A comment may not mean "please fix this sentence so you can keep it." The comment may be there to say, "here is an example of this kind of problem so you can avoid it or fix it in the future." Consulting the comments in the correct order can help you fix the content before fixing the sentence-level problems.

> On another note, remember that TTMA means "Talk To Me About" whatever is noted. Before our conference, please review the paper and mark all TTMA comments *and* any other comments you have questions about. Finally, don't worry if there seem to be a lot of comments; I always comment in detail on this draft.

I use several abbreviations in my comments; I define any that I think may be unfamiliar to the students. The most significant abbreviation is "TTMA," which, as noted above, stands for "Talk To Me About" whatever is noted. For example, I might write "TTMA why you decided to address this issue first." In this way I help to set up the conference by flagging items that I want to discuss with the student. Although the all-caps "TTMA" catches the eye, I ask the student to review my comments and to highlight any "TTMA's" before we meet. I also ask the students to highlight any comments about which they have a question. In this way, I hope to pre-empt those students who want to review every single comment in the conference. (Often, this is a result of not having looked at the paper before the conference.)

a. Content-type comments

In a study that Anne Enquist conducted (*see* Anne Enquist, *Critiquing Law Students' Writing: What the Students Say is Effective*, 2 Legal Writing: J. Legal Writing Inst. 145 (1996)), law students stated that they perceived teachers' comments as "useful" more often when the teachers included either an explanation or an example. I agree with this, although I don't recommend giving an example with *every* comment (you can end up rewriting the paper for the student). When an example is not appropriate, you can try explaining what you mean, or why you believe that the writing doesn't fulfill its purpose. Try to make the reader's comprehension the focal point of the comments. You should also try to explain the reason for reader's misunderstanding whenever possible. E.g., rather than writing "relevance?" say "Reader doesn't understand the relevance of this case because she doesn't know the legally significant facts (or the holding, or the rationale, etc.). <u>See</u> Sample Brief p. XX for examples of effective case descriptions." In this way, you let the writer know what the reader needs, and give the writer resources to help correct the problem.

Citing to relevant pages when commenting can be very helpful. First, many students have a hard time adjusting to legal writing's demand for precision and clarity. If they see legal writing rules (e.g., about stating the conclusion first, or about including facts from relevant case authority) in black and white, they are more likely to believe them. Citing to the text is admittedly a time-consuming process, especially at first, but it pays off. Your comments and the text's guidelines corroborate each other, giving you both added credibility. Whether you are citing to this text or another, I recommend citing to a section (if possible) rather than to a particular page. When a new edition of a text appears, it is unlikely that the material will appear on the same *page*, but it is quite likely that it will be in the same *section*. If you reference sections, you may find that you begin to memorize certain sections for certain references, which can save you time when critiquing.

b. <u>Style and mechanics</u>

Resist the urge to rewrite the assignment for the student. Instead, try to figure out the style or mechanical problem that the student has (is the mistake a typo, or are there similar mistakes throughout?). If you see the problem again and again, you might rewrite once; then, in your final comment, tell the student that you identified a recurring problem and suggest methods for solving the problem, citing to appropriate pages in the texts or to an outside text. If you have time during the conference, you may wish to ask the student to try to use the texts to fix other similar errors.

One particular warning about mechanical problems. It may seem to you that it will be easier to just fix the errors than to write a comment on them. Just fixing them yourself is bad for a couple of reasons. First, you may not notice the *category* of error, and this will make it more difficult to help the student. You might think, as you go to write your final comment, "he had a lot of punctuation errors," and want to write a comment noting that the student should pay more attention to punctuation. But if you go back and analyze the mistakes (or, better, note them as you read), you may realize that there are 2 or 3 specific problems that repeat again and again. Accordingly, your final comment can give more specific advice, e.g., "I noticed that you had several comma splices and several commas missing in sentences with two independent clauses. Consult *Just Writing* at page XX to review the rules for these two problems. We'll talk about it in the conference."

Second, don't even try to mark every "mechanical" problem. Marking these errors confuses students who may need to revise or rewrite before they can edit. As indicated above, you may be thinking, "here is an example of a mistake. Study my correction and apply it to all similar mistakes." Your student may see the correction and think, "she wants me to keep this sentence in the revision because she showed me how to fix it." If grammar and punctuation problems are pervasive, you can try one of two techniques. First, you could rely on a final comment of the type noted above to alert the student to the problem. E.g., "You will be revising this paper, so I didn't mark all of your grammar and punctuation errors. I noticed, however, that many of your complex sentences are difficult for reader to understand. Take a look at the sentences I've marked (I didn't mark all of the problems I found) and bring a legal writing text to our conference so we can talk about it." In the alternative, if the problems are so pervasive that there are many errors on every page, you can try to note each grammatical error in one paragraph or on one page, and then explain to the student that this paragraph or page is an example of the kinds of errors that occur throughout the document.

c.   Accentuate the positive

My permanent New Year's Resolution is to a) make more positive comments on papers, and b) make those positive comments as specific as I make my negative comments. I would never write "bad!" in the margin, yet I frequently write "good!" and think that that's enough. Students need to know what they do right if they are going to repeat it, and I'm trying to make more comments like "The way you echoed the phrase-that-pays really helps reader see how the law and the facts connect." One of my adjuncts wrote all his positive comments in green so that he could review his critiques and tell at a glance whether he had made enough positive comments. Craig Smith, of the University of North Carolina, starts all of his positive comments with "Bravo!" so that students' eyes are drawn to them.

I attended a session at the 2010 LWI conference that was presented by Anthony Niedwiecki of John Marshall and Olympia Duhart of Nova Southeastern. They recommend asking your students to write up a quick evaluation of your critique before the conference, and one of the questions they ask the students to answer is essentially, "based on the critique, what are the strong aspects of this document?" I think this is a great idea and plan to implement it. Whether or not you do, you should be sure to write a critique that makes clear to the student what the strong aspects of the document are

d.   Watch out for your pet peeves!

All writing teachers have pet peeves (one of mine is making sure periods and commas are inside quotation marks). It's fine to point these out and help students to avoid these problems, but (1) make sure you are correct – many pet peeves are the result of a teacher with a similar pet peeve, and not all of our teachers were correct; (2) don't let your attention to the pet peeves distract you from more significant problems that the brief has. In particular, don't let attention to mechanics overshadow attention to substance and structure.

e. Tone

Be careful with your tone when correcting papers. Law students – like all students – can be very sensitive, and a sarcastic comment can cut deep. In addition, some students may not realize that you mean a written comment in jest. In the conference, you can convey humor through your tone of voice, etc., but that doesn't work on paper. I think humor can be used effectively, but I avoid using it in written comments unless I know the student pretty well.

f. **Number of comments**

Generally you should write comments (in the margins or on a separate sheet) reacting to specific concerns that hit you as you read the paper. As I noted above, you may also wish to react to things that the students do correctly. An average of three comments per page is not too many, and many writing teachers comment even more frequently. Of course, not every comment has the same depth or detail. Try to comment specifically about good things (e.g., "Your application is easy to understand because you echoed the phrase-that-pays") and to ask questions about bad things (e.g., "How has this rule been applied in the past?" OR "What's your conclusion based on this analysis?" OR "How does this case support your argument?") Of course, you may use abbrevs. appropriately.

Students do notice it when we mark the first few pages of a paper very thoroughly and the last few pages hardly at all; they also compare papers, and notice if we correct one person's paper more thoroughly than another. While some of the difference may be caused by the different quality of the two papers, ideally, all papers will have thorough comments – a good paper should be thoroughly critiqued because we will have thoroughly explained why it is so good.

I recommend using a criteria sheet of some kind. The sample criteria sheet asks questions about what the paper does or doesn't contain (e.g., sufficient research, strong organization). You may wish to develop your own criteria sheet. By answering the questions on the criteria sheet (yes, no, sometimes, usually, almost never, needs work, not in every section), we give students concrete goals for their revisions.

3. **Writing a final comment**

Anne Enquist's work has also shown that students get much more out of a teacher's written critiques when the teacher has written a final comment. In the final comment, you can provide valuable overall perspective for the student and give the student specific revision goals. Without the final comment, your numerous marginal comments can seem unfocused and overwhelming. For example, even though I do not complete a formal critique of the macro draft (see discussion in notes for Chapter Seven below), I still write a final comment.

To prepare for writing the final comment, you may wish to keep a piece of scrap paper handy while you review the whole paper. As you read, jot down ideas (of both strengths and weaknesses) for the final comment that occur to you. When you're finished with the whole paper, note the most important points that you've written down and review your comments on the entire paper before composing a final comment.

In the final comment, react to the paper as a whole and lay out the agenda for the conference, prioritizing the things you want to talk about. Because you probably won't have time in the conference to discuss every problem in the paper, you should pick the 2-4 most significant problems for discussion. When choosing them, think about what problems the student may be able to solve alone by using the texts (with your references) and what problems need to be talked out. You might end your comment by saying something like this: "In our conference, make sure to talk to me about (1) using more detail when describing significant authority cases, (2) reaching a conclusion in each section, and, most importantly, (3) your large-scale organization."

> NOTE: I recommend that you write a detailed final comment even if you must hand the paper back to the student during the conference. You may think that you'll remember what you wanted to say to each student, but it's very easy to forget. Writing a detailed final comment ensures that you have something definite to talk about with each student, and gives you a quick overview of the paper. You might even write the final comment at least in part with your own needs in mind – what strengths and "things to work on" (better than "weaknesses") can you point out in the final comment that will remind you about this paper?

When composing the final comment, strive to find something nice to say. With most papers this task will be easy; with some it will be very difficult. Most students have at least a general idea of the right law and a general understanding of the legal issue(s). Praise them for their understanding and their identification of the correct legal standards and/or legally significant facts. I often write something like one of the following:

> A. "I can see that you understand the issues here; you've done a good job of identifying the legally significant facts, and you've cited almost all of the relevant legal standards. Let's work on a way to better communicate your understanding to the reader. In our conference . . . ."

> B. "You've done a good job for your client. You found all the right law, and you know how it applies in this case. You need to work on doing a good job for the reader, so that she can easily understand all the great stuff you've found out. In our conference . . . ."

Anne Enquist's research has also revealed the importance to students of positive feedback. Many students do not have "the will to go on" unless they receive some positive feedback; feedback that is exclusively negative can make them feel that they've done everything wrong and that they shouldn't bother even trying to revise.

As noted above, I tell my students to note the priority level of comments, and I tell them specifically that they should review the comments and highlight the ones that I want to talk about (as signaled by "TTMA" comments) and that they want to talk about.

In this way, I ensure that the students arrive at the conference with several comments highlighted. I start the conference by reviewing my final comment and discussing any issues raised in that comment. We then move to the highlighted comments. This method prevents most students from insisting on going through each comment – it saves precious conference time for only those comments that were significant, confusing, or both. See notes below for more information about conferences.

4.   Scoring the Macro & Micro Drafts

If you use the scoring method recommended on the criteria sheets, you may assign a score between 0 and -15 for the macro and micro drafts. Remember that any points you take off of this draft will come off the student's score for the final draft. Therefore, if you deduct lots of points on one or two students' drafts only, you may make it mathematically impossible for those students to get an "A" on the brief (even if you curve). To avoid this problem, make sure that there are not one or two outliers who have lost a lot of points. For example, it might be appropriate if most of your papers have no more than four points taken off, and if many have zero points taken off.

When reviewing research, organization, and analysis, look for a good faith effort to meet the requirements of the criteria sheet. If they essentially met the requirements, but fell down or neglected only one or two items, you may decide to take zero points off. I base my decisions on the impact that the problem had on the paper as a whole, and the amount of work evident in the draft as a whole.

On the other hand, I don't feel pressured to take zero points off; it is perfectly appropriate to knock a couple of points off the draft if the student has not put forth a good faith effort. It's a judgment call; being a little generous is fine, but if I am "too" generous, the students who worked hard feel like they were being chumps (although the hard workers tend to do well on the final draft). The main thing is to be consistent in your standards from student to student.

1.   Returning the Papers

Plan your syllabus and your critiquing schedule to allow you to return papers at least one day before the conference. If you do not return the papers until the conference, the student will spend the conference frantically trying to read your comments and evaluating the significance of the points taken off or the score, no matter how carefully you have planned the time. Thus, you should strive to give the students their papers at least 24 hours before the planned conference time, if not before then. I tell my students when to expect their papers, and inform them that they should budget some time to review the paper before our conference. I also keep a copy of the paper so that I can review my comments during the conference without having to take the paper from the student.

Ideally, the papers should be returned to the students a day or two before the conference so that they can review your comments before the conference. If this is not possible, tell the students to check their mailboxes *one hour* before the conference. (Of course, you will have made sure that you returned the papers to all of the students an hour before the conferences begin.) In that way, they can spend time *before* the conference reviewing the paper. Conferences do not go well when the student is spending the whole time trying to read and assimilate comments while pretending to pay attention to your discussion.

6. In the conference

During the conference, try not to do all the talking yourself. As a general rule, *the more the student talks, the more the student learns.* Avoid telling the student how to rewrite a particular section. Instead, start by asking the student how they felt about particular aspects of the paper. If a student starts out by admitting a problem, the conference will usually go more smoothly. In the alternative, if you have to bring up a concern, you can ask the student what guideline applies (you can give them the text and have them read about the guideline if need be) and ask them how they might go about rewriting or revising.

When asked to revise on the spot, students will typically look down at what they've already written, and may end up "massaging the mistake." I frequently put my hand over what they've written, or turn the paper over, and just ask about the point we're discussing, e.g., "What is your client's best argument?" Frequently the answer is more specific than what's in the paper, and the student realizes that he or she could have written it better.

The more demands you make of the students during the conferences, the more they will learn. As a way of keeping the student involved, you can ask for the student's questions, or ask what the student liked or didn't like about his or her paper.

At the end of the conference you should review your accomplishments. Ask the students what specific things they are going to do to improve the next draft. Reviewing in this way lets you find out whether the student learned what you intended to teach. I know some teachers who BEGIN the conference by asking the students what they think they need to work on for the next draft, or what they're most concerned about, etc. This method can help ensure student participation, as well as ensuring that you get to the point that's bugging the student the most.

Sample syllabi follow. They of course contain many specifics that apply only to my own course, but I include them because they may mirror items that all teachers might include in their own syllabi.

APPELLATE ADVOCACY
Sample Syllabus

I. <u>Course Materials</u>

<u>Mandatory</u>:
Beazley, <u>A Practical Guide to Appellate Advocacy</u> (Aspen, 3d ed. 2010) (<u>APG</u>)
A citation manual
Pink, green, blue, and yellow highlighters
3 Binder clips for 20-40 page documents

May be recommended *as needed*:
Anne Enquist & Laurel Currie Oates, <u>Just Writing</u> (Aspen, 3d ed. 2009)

II. <u>Course Requirements</u>

Attendance is required. Points may be deducted from the final grade for failure to attend class regularly, for failure to arrive at class on time or to stay for the entire class, for web-surfing or messaging during class, or for failure to turn papers in on time without a valid extension. General grading criteria are explained below. Each adjunct's section is graded separately; no student is ever compared to a student who has a different adjunct for purposes of determining grades. Although I reserve the right to make changes, the final grade in Law 600 will most likely be drawn from the following elements:

75%   Final Draft, Appellate Brief
The final grade on the Appellate Brief takes into account points deducted from the macro and micro drafts and points deducted for failure to attend conferences. The grade also takes into account performance on self-grading and in the conferences. *Dicta grades are NOT taken into account when the final grade is awarded and are NOT necessarily predictors of the final grade.*

5%   Class participation
The class participation grade takes into account attendance, homework completion, and scores on any quizzes. Students may be counted absent if they use computers for purposes other than note-taking or approved class participation.

20%   Oral Arguments
Each student will participate in at least one practice argument (judged by 3-L students) and one performance argument (graded by the adjunct). The score for the performance argument may take the practice argument into account.

III. <u>Adjuncts</u>

Each student in Appellate Advocacy is required to meet several times with an Adjunct Professor during the semester. I will schedule the initial adjunct group meeting; the other meetings will be **as scheduled** by the adjunct and students, and will not necessarily be the same night as the original meeting. These meetings will usually occur during evenings and weekends. Group meeting times will be posted on the course website and on the assignment board; students schedule individual conferences directly with the adjunct and are responsible for keeping track of their own schedules. Adjunct names and e-mail addresses can be found on the course website.

IV. **Honor Code Requirements**

Plagiarism

Sections (B)(2), (3), and (4) of Article IV of the Honor Code of the Ohio State University College of Law provide:

> 2. When the relevant instructor or competition rules prohibit aid or assistance, no student who knows or should know of the prohibition shall knowingly give or receive aid or assistance in any work in
> a. Any course, seminar, or other offering of the Moritz College of Law.
> b. Any application, competition, or other process to gain a position on a journal, a moot court team, or any other team or group sponsored by, reporting to, or representing the College, whether or not for credit or financial compensation, or
> c. Any intramural or extramural competition of a law-related nature.
>
> 3. No student shall plagiarize
> a. In any written work assigned for any course or seminar,
> b. In any work for any intramural or extramural competition of a law-related nature.
> c. In any journal sponsored by the College, or
> d. In any written work by the student as part of an application, competition, or other process to gain a position on a journal, a moot court team or any other team or group sponsored by, reporting to, or representing the College, whether or not for credit or financial compensation.
>
> Plagiarism means knowingly copying or imitating the ideas or expressions of another and representing them as one's own. Failure to acknowledge or cite a source which is copied or imitated constitutes the representation that the idea or expression is one's own.
>
> 4. No student shall knowingly steal, destroy or impede another student's academic work. Impeding another student's work includes, but is not limited to, the theft, concealment, defacement, or mutilation of common academic resources so that access and use by others is impeded.

Article V, Section C sets forth the procedure that must be followed when a student believes that a violation has occurred:

> Section C. A student who believes that a violation of the Honor Code has occurred shall promptly report his or her belief and the underlying information to

the Associate Dean for Academic Affairs, or, in his/her absence, any member of the full-time faculty of the Moritz College of Law.

Thus, whenever you use the words or ideas of another writer, you should acknowledge the original source. Never copy from a law review or any other material without citing the source properly. If you use the exact words from a source, use quotation marks in addition to citing the source; if you put ideas from a source into your own words, cite the source without using quotation marks. If you are unsure about whether or not you are plagiarizing, or if you are having difficulties with an assignment, talk with your adjunct or with me before turning in the assignment.

Individual Work

Although we may do some group work in class, and although you may conduct research with your classmates as directed, *all writing must be done independently in order to comply with Article IV, Section B(2) of the honor code. Accordingly, no one other than your adjunct may proofread or critique your writing unless your adjunct has given permission.*

Attorney Work Product:

Because we are using real cases pending before the Supreme Court, some or all of the briefs may be available on-line or through other sources. **You are forbidden to consult, in any manner, any attorney work product related or relevant to your case. "Attorney work product" includes but is not limited to: (1) in-house memos or other materials prepared by counsel or their representatives at any stage of the proceedings, or (2) Petitions for Certiorari, Briefs, or Amicus Briefs submitted to the U.S. Supreme Court or any other court at any stage of the litigation. You are also forbidden to consult with any person (other than your adjunct) with knowledge of attorney work product related or relevant to your case. A violation of this requirement will be considered a violation of the Honor Code.** If in doubt, consult with me or with your adjunct *before* consulting the new resource. And, of course, you should cite as needed to any authority you consult.

V. **Late Papers**

Due dates for all three drafts of the brief are noted on the schedule. *Turn all assignments in twice:* (1) a digital version of the draft should be deposited in the TWEN assignment drop box **and** (2) a hard copy of the draft should be turned in as directed, either to me (in class) or to the appropriate box in room 255. Hard copies of drafts will be accepted only if the appropriate criteria sheet (distributed in class and available on the website) is attached, and the correct number of copies is turned in. Some adjuncts may impose additional filing requirements, and you may lose points if you fail to meet these requirements. NOTE: Except for the final draft, due dates vary by section.

The rules about late papers in Appellate Advocacy are strict:

Points may be deducted from your final grade for any papers or assignments turned in after the deadline without the adjunct's permission. In addition, if any draft is more than one week late without a valid excuse, **you will receive a failing grade in the course**. Exceptions will be made only in extremely unusual circumstances. All exceptions must be approved by me *and* the Associate Dean for Academic Affairs (or his or her designee).

Accordingly, you should learn to budget your time so that you complete your assignments before they are due. Be aware of the possibility of equipment failure (e.g., word processor problems, backup on the Lexis and Westlaw computers in the law library) when scheduling your work so you are not left scrambling at the last minute. If you put off completing your assignment until shortly before it is due, you run the risk of equipment failure or other logistical problems, and you may have to suffer the penalty.

Accommodations for Illness or Disability

Accommodation of disability and extensions for illness should be requested before the paper is due and must be requested before it is turned in. I cannot change a grade after the fact based on speculation that the student might have done better if the disability or the illness had not existed. It is best if we are aware of these situations as soon as possible. If you need to request an extension or other accommodation, you may begin the process by talking to your adjunct, to me, to Dean Smith or her designee, or to the University's Office of Disability Services (ODS). Because privacy is often desired in these situations, any necessary documentation can be submitted to ODS or to Dean Smith or her designee, who can maintain your privacy and inform me only of the appropriate accommodation.

VI. **Assignments**

Written Assignments & Reading Assignments:

In this course, you have one major project – the completion of an appellate brief. During the semester, you will complete two kinds of out-of-class work that will help you complete that project: Required Drafts and Homework. Due dates for the three Required Drafts of the brief are noted below and on the website. You must turn in *both* hard copies and digital copies of all three drafts; for some drafts, you must turn in multiple hard copies. Most Homework can be submitted electronically to the course website. If the website is not functioning, you may submit the homework via e-mail, but it will not be counted unless you use the following Subject Header: Homework Section 600 [fill in appropriate section designation]-[fill in date]. E.g., "Homework Section 600LR10 - 09/18/09." Homework assignments are due by 8:00 a.m. on the day *before* your assigned class day unless I tell you otherwise. Note that the due dates for all assignments except the final draft may vary by class day.

Most reading assignments are contained in the syllabus; some may be announced in class. Please consult the course website and the assignment board and check your e-mail periodically so that you are aware of adjunct assignments, oral argument schedules, changes to the schedule, etc.

VII. <u>General Grading Criteria</u>

Your grade on the appellate brief will be based on research and analysis (identification of correct legal issues, accurate and thorough use of appropriate authorities to argue for the resolution of those legal issues), organization (logic, focus, proper paragraph structure, clarity of argument, signals to the reader), style (correct and appropriate sentence structure, word choice, precision, conciseness), and mechanics (grammar, spelling, citation skills). Although you will be given specific criteria at each stage of the writing process, the descriptions below, adapted from a model provided by the University of North Carolina Center for Teaching and Learning, will give you some idea of the reasons behind the grade that you earn on the final draft.

An 'A' brief will make a supervising attorney or judge feel good about relying on your work with little or no revision. A judge would feel confident in basing the reasoning for a judicial opinion on your brief, and a supervising attorney could submit this brief with no more than minor revisions and some discussion with you to be assured that the research was accurate. A supervising attorney or judge would look forward to seeing your work in the future.

<u>An 'A' appellate brief will:</u>

(a) be easy to read due to strong large-scale organization, clarity, and focus;
(b) have no faulty logic or irrational arguments;
(c) argue powerfully and persuasively for your position;
(d) be based on complete and accurate research;
(e) make accurate and effective use of the facts;
(f) make accurate and effective use of relevant sources of law;
(g) use case law accurately and effectively to explain or illustrate legal rules in a meaningful way;
(h) make use of all valid and appropriate arguments, whether based on law, policy, or equity;
(i) follow appellate brief format with no major errors;
(j) have few or no conspicuous citation errors, avoid unnecessary string citations, use citation signals and parentheticals appropriately, and use unobtrusive citations;
(k) be free of errors in grammar, spelling, syntax, and typing.

A 'B' brief will positively impress the supervising attorney or judge and make the judge curious to talk with you further about your work. A judge would feel confident in using your brief as a basis for further research or might ask the law clerk to verify your position. A supervising attorney would enjoy watching your growth and would feel confident that with guidance you will become a very good attorney. A judge would look forward to watching you develop in the future.

A 'B' appellate brief will:

(a) be similar to, but lack the thoroughness, power, or polish of an 'A' brief;

(b) be generally well-organized, but may require the reader to expend more effort or re-read certain sections in order to fully grasp the author's point;

(c) be complete, but may also not use all of the best available legal arguments or authorities, or may not use them as effectively as in an 'A' brief;

(d) be generally well-written, but may also be wordy or contain poor word choice or distracting paragraphing style in some parts of the brief;

(e) capture the judge's attention, but fail to fully persuade;

(f) contain only one or two major citation errors, but may not use signals as effectively, or may use needless string citations or have other citation problems;

(g) contain few if any errors in grammar, spelling, syntax, and typing.

A 'C' brief will make supervising attorneys or judges uneasy about relying unguardedly on your work, and may make them feel uncomfortable with work that you submit in the future. A judge might pick up some interesting points from the brief, but would feel compelled to rethink the legal reasoning and/or closely examine your research. A supervising attorney would not be comfortable submitting the brief to a court without making fairly major changes in the style, tone, or content. However, a supervising attorney would see sufficient promise in your work to be motivated to invest time and energy in supervising your future assignments more closely, and a judge would feel that you had made a conscientious effort to argue your client's case.

A 'C' appellate brief may:

(a) be similar to, but lack the thoroughness, power, or polish of a 'B' brief;

(b) present some good thoughts, but contain noticeable paragraphing or organizational errors;

(c) fail to present a legally plausible argument or present a plausible argument ineffectively;

(d) fail to include some or most of the best available arguments or authorities;

(e) rely upon authority whose relevance is not immediately apparent, and fail to provide an explanation of the authority's relevance and weight;

(f) fail to accurately explain the meaning of legal authorities;

(g) contain major errors in acceptable format;

(h) contain more numerous errors in grammar, spelling, syntax, or typing;

(j) contain a series of major citation errors.

A 'D' brief will not be acceptable to judges or supervising attorneys. It may provide a few cases or ideas from which they could begin on their own, but would be wholly undependable standing alone. A supervising attorney would need to rework the document or assign it to a different associate. A judge might consider sanctions if this brief were submitted by a practicing attorney. Both a judge and a supervising attorney might question the reliability of future work of an attorney who submitted this brief.

A 'D' appellate brief may:

(a) significantly misrepresent the facts, legal authorities, or major legal issues;

(b) significantly fail to use the relevant facts or legal authorities within the argument, may present significant arguments with little or no factual or legal support, or may fail to include significant arguments or major legal issues;

(c) contain so many paragraphing or organizational errors (or both) as to prohibit the reader from following the writer's thoughts;

(d) conspicuously fail to follow required format;

(e) contain many errors in grammar, spelling, or typing;

(f) contain more illogical, implausible, and irrational arguments than acceptable arguments;

(g) demonstrate no effort to use correct citation format.

An 'F' brief will miss the point of the assignment entirely and/or show a lack of good faith effort to complete the assignment.

SCHEDULE [for eleven weeks of class meetings]

[Homework assignments shown in brackets are not included on my syllabus, but are posted on the course website, announced in class, or both.]

Week One

APG chs. 1-3.

In class: intro material and information; research methods; records distributed

[Please finish reading your record, including any decisions below. Please bring a printed/written copy of the following to class:

1. Identify at least 3 facts that might be significant to your side's argument.
2. Identify the two most significant authorities you are aware of to date (these may be from the lower court decision or may be things you have found on your own). Be able to explain why they are significant.
3. Identify at least 3 specific avenues for research (e.g., shepardize/keycite X case from lower court decision, look for law review article about Z, look for Supreme Court cases in Q area). Be able to explain your choices.
4. Identify at least 3 legal/factual/policy categories that you might fit the case into.

E.g., the issue in the Chickasaw Nation case was how to interpret a tax law that applied to Indian tribes. 3 categories might be: tax law, laws/policies dealing with native American issues, and statutory construction issues.

If you do not have these items in writing, you will be turned away from the class with an unexcused absence.[1]

---

[1]As indicated above, some teachers are concerned that a requirement of this type inhibits student learning; some people think that a requirement like this constitutes a "power play" on the part of the teacher. I recognize that this demand may result in a student being turned away from a learning opportunity. However, out of 750 students, I have had only two students show up without completing the work. I think the written work demanded is simple enough that it can be completed in five or ten minutes before class (and in fact, I have seen students in line on their way into class completing – or starting and completing – the written part of the assignment). The payoff in class participation has been extraordinary. If you are concerned about the "no admittance" requirement, there are at least two alternatives: (1) require students to complete the reading before class, and then take class time to ask them to do

Week Two

APG chs.3-4. Read and abstract your record; prepare homework as instructed, submit electronically by 7:30 a.m. of class day, **and bring a copy to class (required for admission)**. In class: research methods; standards of review; introduction to argument

Adjunct work: **Complete Homework for and attend adjunct organizational meeting.** Adjunct sections will be posted by Monday of this week. Organizational meetings will be held on Tuesday or Wednesday.

Week Three

APG chs. 5-6; review Sample Briefs. **Submit one annotated outline or "CREXAC unit of discourse" from argument (due on course website the day before class at 8:00 a.m.).**

> [Make tentative outline to identify units of discourse over weekend. Draft an outline **OR** at least one "crexac unit of discourse" (as defined in the text). Turn in to the course website by 8:00 a.m. the day before class day.]

In class: Drafting the Argument
Adjunct work: as scheduled

Week Four

APG chapter 7; review class notes
In class: Effective use of Authority; self-grading; bring highlighters to class
Due date: Macro draft due on course website at 11:55 the night before class; in class, turn in hard copy with criteria sheet attached.
Adjunct work: as scheduled

Week Five

APG ch. 9; review Sample Briefs as assigned. **Submit one question presented with description of persuasive techniques as assigned (due on course website the day before class at 8:00 a.m.).**

> [Draft at least one question presented for your case. Use one or more of the persuasive writing techniques described in chapter 9, and explain which methods you used and why. NOTE: you must identify a persuasive writing technique other than choosing the "under-does-when" v. the "whether" structure for your question.)]

In class: Questions Presented, Statement of the Case, Summary of the Argument
Adjunct work: Conferences as scheduled

---

the written preparation; (2) require students to e-mail you the written work by 8:00 a.m. on the morning of the class meeting and to bring a copy to class. Even if they forget the copy, they will still have done the needed thinking to prepare them for the class session.

Week Six
APG chs.8 & 10 & U.S. Supreme Court rules as assigned; review Sample Briefs as noted. **Bring current copy of argument section to class. Submit Kevin Bacon strings on course website as assigned.**
In class: Appellate Brief Formalities; making your brief reader-friendly
Adjunct work: Conferences if scheduled

Week Seven
APG ch. 13 & Appendix A.1-A.4; review <u>BB</u> as needed.
In class: Citation Form Review; Intro. to Oral Argument. Please bring bluebook to class.
Due date: Micro draft due on course website at 11:55 the night before class; in class, turn in <u>two</u> hard copies: one copy for your adjunct, with criteria sheet attached, and one copy for your opponent(s), with opponent name(s) written in the <u>upper right-hand corner</u> of the brief.)
Adjunct work: As scheduled

Week Eight
APG ch. 13 & § 14.5.
In class: Oral Argument
Adjunct work: Adjunct Conference as scheduled

Week Nine
APG chs. 5-6, 10-11; **bring copy of case description(s) to class (as assigned during Week Eight; you may bring case description from current draft of your brief)**
> [Ticket of admission to class: Assigned case description. (Bringing a copy of your brief to class will fulfill this requirement, as long as your brief includes a description of the assigned case.)][2]
In class: Focused revision techniques
Adjunct work: Adjunct conference and/or practice argument as scheduled

Week Ten
APG chs. 11-12; Appendix § A.5
In class: Revision & Polishing Techniques.
Adjunct work: Adjunct conference and/or practice argument as scheduled

Week Eleven
APG: review ch. 13 & § 14.5

---

[2]As noted below, one technique to use for this class is to show the impact of positions of emphasis by having students work on effective topic sentences in the rule explanation section of the argument. To do this, I identify a case that all the petitioners and/or all the respondents will or should be discussing. I ask them to bring a case description of that case to class (as indicated, many just bring a page from or a copy of their in-process brief). In class, we first review effective case descriptions and have the students work in groups to write up an effective description of the case. This is followed by having the students write an effective topic sentence to put "on top of" the case.

In class: Oral Argument wrap-up; course evaluations
Due Dates: For all sections, digital copy of Final Draft due on the course website at 9:00 p.m. on <u>Sunday</u>. <u>Three hard copies</u> of Final Draft due by 8:00 a.m. <u>on Monday</u> (<u>All Sections</u>) (The three hard copies: One copy for your adjunct (with criteria sheet attached) and two copies for the judges.) **Students are encouraged to take advantage of early turn-in at the library desk over the weekend.**
Serve copy of brief on opponent as instructed in class.

<u>Weeks Twelve - Fourteen</u>
One performance argument as scheduled, weeks 12-14.

<u>SCHEDULE</u> [for 14 weeks of class meetings and one week of oral arguments]
[See eleven week schedule for extra information re: homework assignments]

<u>Week One</u>
Read <u>APG</u> Chapters 1-2; § 3.1
In class: intro material and information; research methods; records distributed

<u>Week Two</u>
Read and abstract your record; <u>APG</u> §§ 3.2-3.3
In class: research methods; standards of review

<u>Week Three</u>
Review Sample Briefs as assigned; read <u>APG</u> Chapter 4
In class: Planning the argument: creating an outline

<u>Week Four</u>
Review Sample Briefs as assigned; read <u>APG</u> Chapter 5
In class: Drafting the Argument

<u>Week Five</u>
Read <u>APG</u> Chapter 6
In class: Using case authority effectively
<u>Week Six</u>
Read <u>APG</u> Chapter 7
In class: Effective use of authority; self-grading; bring copy of Macro and highlighters to class
Due date: Macro draft due at 8:30 a.m. <u>one day before</u> scheduled class meeting day (Please turn in one copy and keep one copy)

<u>Week Seven</u>
Read <u>APG</u> Chapters 8-9; Appendix B; review Sample Briefs as assigned
In class: Appellate Brief Formalities; Questions Presented
Conferences as scheduled

Week Eight
Review APG chapter 9, Appendix B
In class: Statement of the Case; Summary of the Argument, Effective Point Headings

Week Nine
Read APG Chapter 10; review Sample Briefs as noted
In class: Making your brief reader-friendly
Conferences as scheduled

Week Ten
Complete cite form worksheet; review Citation Manual as needed; Read APG Appendix A.1-
    A.4; Chapter 13
In class: Citation Form Review; Intro. to Oral Argument
**Due date: Micro Draft due at 8:30 a.m. <u>one day before</u> scheduled class day (Please turn in
    two copies)**

Week Eleven
Review APG Chapter 13; read APG § 14.5
In class: Oral Argument
Conference as scheduled

Week Twelve
Read APG Chapter 11
In class: Persuasive Writing Techniques
Practice argument as scheduled

Week Thirteen
Read APG Chapter 12; Appendix A, § A.5
In class: Revising and Polishing Methods

Week Fourteen
Review APG Chapter 13 & § 14.5
Oral Argument wrap up; course evaluations
Due Dates: Final Drafts due at 8:30 a.m. <u>on scheduled class day</u> (Please turn in five copies)

Week Fifteen
One performance argument as scheduled Mon.-Sat.

Fill in your name and then attach this sheet to the top of your ANNOTATED OUTLINE and turn both in together on the due date.

STUDENT:_____

CRITERIA SHEET
APPELLATE ADVOCACY

ANNOTATED OUTLINE (Max. = 0; Min. = -15)_____
> [The final draft will be scored on a 65-point scale. Points deducted here will be deducted from that 65 points.]

I.   MINIMUM REQUIREMENTS

A.   Does the outline include the following sections, in order? 1) Standard of Review, 2) Working Headings, 3) Rule(s), 4) Support. Has the writer followed the guidelines for each of the sections?

B.   Is the document neatly typed and paginated, with adequate margins, and is this sheet attached with the student's name filled in?

G.   Did the writer include appropriate private memo notes?

II.   STANDARD OF REVIEW

Did the writer accurately identify the standard(s) of review for the issue(s) before the Court and provide appropriate authority for the standard(s)?

III.   WORKING HEADINGS

A.   In working headings and sub-headings, did the writer accurately identify all or most of the assertions that he or she wants to convince the court to agree with in order to prevail?

B.   Are the headings and sub-headings built around the issues and sub-issues that the case presents? Are they presented in a logical order?

IV.   RULE OR OTHER THESIS

Within each unit of discourse identified by headings or sub-headings, did the writer accurately identify or formulate the relevant legal rules that could or would apply? If a unit of discourse is focused on a thesis other than a rule, did the writer articulate that thesis?

V.   SUPPORT

A.   Within each heading or sub-heading, did the writer list all or most of the significant authorities that could be used to support, explain, or illustrate each rule or thesis?

B.   For each authority listed, did the writer include a short, accurate, explanation?

C.   Did the writer include full citation information for each authority listed as support?

Fill in your name and your adjunct's name, sign honor code pledge, and attach this document to your MACRO DRAFT. Turn it in at the beginning of class (after having filed the brief electronically the night before). You will need an extra copy of your brief to complete the self-grading exercise, due in the conference.

Student:_____

CRITERIA SHEET
MACRO DRAFT & SELF-GRADING CONFERENCE

Score (to be given after conference; Max. = 0; Min. = -15) _____

[The final draft of the Appellate Brief will be given a raw score on a 65-point scale. Points taken off this draft will be taken off that 65 points. The dicta grade is not necessarily a predictor of the final grade and will not be taken into account when determining the final grade. Do not rely on the dicta grade.]

I. Professionalism

A. Format

Has the writer included an argument section that meets the criteria noted in Parts II-III below? Does the writer use headings to divide the Argument into focused analytical segments?

B. Private Memos (See Class Notes & Text, § 4.2)

Has the writer used footnotes or marginal notes and an end comment to 1) identify and explain the strongest parts of the document, 2) ask for specific help on certain parts of the document, and 3) identify any experiments or innovations the writer tried?

C. Self-Grading: Has the writer turned in a clean copy of the draft and brought a self-graded copy and a rule/focus list to the conference? Is the writer able to discuss the brief as noted in Part IV below? (See Ch. 7 & class notes)

D. Is the document neatly typed, double-spaced, and paginated, and did the writer turn the paper in on time with this document attached to it? Is there evidence of basic spell-checking and proofreading? Are typographical errors corrected neatly in pen?

II. Research & Issue Identification

Did the writer identify all or most of the relevant legal issues and sub-issues within the Argument?

Did the writer identify all or most of the significant authorities (i.e., applicable statutes, significant cases, etc.) relevant to each issue? Did the writer identify other authorities and sources needed for the argument?

If appropriate, has the writer gone beyond the authorities cited in the record and cases below to more recent authorities and/or to authorities more appropriate for a Supreme Court Brief?

III. Argument: Organization & Legal Analysis

Did the writer organize the Argument around the identified issues and sub-issues, or organize the Argument in some other manner that allows the reader to understand easily how the authorities and arguments relate to the case?

Did the writer address the strongest issue first or follow some other logical method of ordering the issues (e.g., discussing a threshold issue first)?

Does each section or sub-section within the argument focus on an applicable rule, sub-rule, policy, or other thesis?

Does the writer adequately explain the meaning and/or the significance of the rule or thesis that is the focus of each section?

Did the writer cite the significant authorities (i.e., applicable statutes, significant cases, etc.) relevant to each issue? Did the writer avoid citing (a) irrelevant authorities and (b) authorities inappropriate for a Supreme Court brief?

Did the writer provide enough information about each significant authority so that the reader was able to understand its relevance to the writer's analysis? (e.g., quoting and explaining the important portions of significant statutes; identifying the relevant issue(s), disposition(s), facts, and reasoning of significant cases.)

Does the argument clarify why the Court should accept the writer's arguments on each issue as opposed to the other side's?

Within each section or sub-section of the argument, does the writer explicitly show the connection between the case before the court and the rule, sub-rule, or other thesis? (i.e., does the writer apply the rule or thesis to the facts?)

Did the writer explicitly end the discussion of each issue and sub-issue by stating the conclusion as to the issue under discussion and, as needed, connecting that issue to the overall thesis?

IV. Conference Preparation and Participation

Did the writer complete the required self-grading before the conference? (See class notes and workshop)

Did the writer bring the self-graded copy of the draft <u>and</u> the rule/focus list to the conference? Did the writer bring any other necessary materials to the conference? (e.g., course materials, additions or corrections to the brief, etc.)

Was the writer able to participate fully in the conference by taking the adjunct through any section or sub-section of the argument and discussing the relevant analytical elements? If the writer has made additions or corrections to the draft after self-grading, is he or she able to explain why those additions or corrections were necessary and how they change the document?

Was the writer able to answer reasonable questions about the case and about the draft? Did the writer have a good grasp of the facts and issues of the client's case and of the significant authorities relevant to the client's case?

V. Certification

I sign below to certify that I have complied with the honor code and the rules for this course noted in the syllabus, including but not limited to 1) writing the brief independently, and 2) not consulting briefs or other student or attorney work product related to this case.

_____

Student Signature

STUDENT:_____

<u>FINAL COMMENT</u>
No critique can or should identify every possible writing and/or analytical problem. To receive the best possible score in any area on the final draft, however, the writer should note the revision level suggested below when revising.

A. CONTENT & ORGANIZATION (including research & presentation of issues)
COMMENTS:

   ___Significant revision needed ___throughout___as noted
   ___Moderate revision needed ___throughout ___ as noted
   ___Minimal revision needed ___throughout ___as noted
   ___Don't touch it

B. LEGAL ANALYSIS (including rule articulation, explanation (discussion of authority cases) and application of law to facts)
COMMENTS:

   ___Significant revision needed ___throughout___as noted
   ___Moderate revision needed ___throughout ___ as noted
   ___Minimal revision needed ___throughout___as noted
   ___Don't touch it

C. WRITING STYLE (including small-scale organization & sentence structure)
COMMENTS:

   ___Significant revision needed ___throughout___as noted
   ___Moderate revision needed ___throughout ___ as noted
   ___Minimal revision needed ___throughout ___as noted
   ___Don't touch it

D. MECHANICS (including grammar, punctuation, & citation form)
COMMENTS:

   ___Significant revision needed ___throughout___as noted
   ___Moderate revision needed ___throughout ___ as noted
   ___Minimal revision needed ___throughout ___as noted
   ___Don't touch it

OTHER COMMENTS:

File the digital copy of your paper by 11:55 p.m. on the night before class. Attach this criteria sheet to the Micro draft and bring to class as assigned. Bring a SECOND copy of the brief cover page + argument section only for your opponent.

STUDENT:_____

MICRO DRAFT CRITERIA SHEET

Score (Max. = 0; Min. = -15) _____   Dicta Grade:_____ [optional]
    [The final draft of the Appellate Brief will be given a raw score on a 65-point scale. Points taken off this draft will be taken off that 65 points.]

I. Professionalism
A. Does the document include the following elements, formatted correctly? 1) Cover Sheet, 2) Question(s) Presented, 3) Parties to the Proceeding (if needed), 4) Table of Contents, 5) Table of Authorities, 6) Opinions Below, 7) Jurisdiction, 8) Constitutional and/or Statutory Provisions Involved (if needed), 9) Standard of Review, 10) Statement of the Case, 11) Summary of the Argument, 12) Argument, 13) Conclusion, 14) Signature Block, 15) Appendix (if needed), 16) Certificate of Service, 17) Certificate of Compliance with signed honor code certification. (See also Course materials, Class notes, APG ch. 8, & APG Appendixes.)

B. Question(s) Presented (See APG ch. 9) Has the writer included appropriate question(s) presented? Does each question appropriately reflect the writer's theme? Does each question avoid assuming elements at issue and avoid other problems?

C. Standard of Review (See APG ch. 2) Does the writer identify the correct appellate standard of review? Does the writer cite appropriate authority for the standard?

D. Statement of the Case (See APG ch. 9) Does the Statement 1) begin with context, 2) include the procedural and factual history of the case, 3) include cites to the record, 4) use persuasive techniques appropriately and effectively, and 5) include only honest and accurate information?

E. Summary of the Argument (See APG ch. 9) Does the summary provide a concise roadmap OR an argumentative overview of the argument, using case and statutory citations only as appropriate?

F. Argument & Point Headings (See APG chs. 5-9) Has the writer included an argument section that meets the criteria noted in Parts II-III below? Within the argument, are the Point Headings argumentative sentences that make specific points about the writer's argument, and do they divide the argument into appropriate CREXAC units of discourse?

G. Conclusion/Signature Block (See APG ch. 8) Has the writer explicitly told the court to grant the appropriate relief? (e.g., "this Court should affirm/reverse. . .") If more information is included, has the writer focused the conclusion? Did the writer sign the Certificate of Compliance and include other signature blocks as needed?

H. Appendix (See APG ch. 8) Has the writer included an appendix only if needed? If needed, does the appendix include appropriate legislation or other materials?

I. Private Memo (See Class notes) Has the writer used footnotes or marginal notes and an end comment to 1) identify the strongest parts of the document and explain their strengths, 2) ask for specific help on certain parts of the document?

J. Is the document double-spaced and paginated? Were digital and hard copies turned in on time with this sheet attached to the hard copy? Are typographical errors corrected neatly in pen?

II. Research & Issue Identification

Did the writer identify all of the relevant legal issues and sub-issues within the Argument? Does the writer make all or most of the best arguments available?

Did the writer cite appropriate authority for each legal proposition?

Did the writer support the arguments made with all or most of the best authorities (i.e., applicable statutes, significant cases, etc.) relevant to each issue?

Did the writer avoid overstating the strength or weakness of the relevant authorities and facts?

If appropriate, has the writer gone beyond the authorities cited in the record to more recent authorities and/or to authorities more appropriate for a Supreme Court Brief?

Did the writer avoid irrelevant issues and arguments without valid support?

III. Argument: Organization & Legal Analysis

Did the writer organize the Argument around the identified issues and sub-issues, or organize the Argument in some other manner that allows the reader to understand easily how the authorities and arguments relate to the case? Did the writer address the strongest issue first or follow another logical method of ordering the issues (e.g., discussing a threshold issue first)?

Does the writer reconcile any seemingly inconsistent arguments?

Does each section or sub-section within the argument focus on an applicable rule, sub-rule, policy, or other thesis? Does the writer make clear how each point connects to the rule(s) that govern the case or to the brief's main thesis?

Did the writer adequately explain the significance of the rule or thesis that is the focus of each section? Unless circumstances dictated otherwise, did the writer finish explaining the rule *before* applying it to the facts?

When explaining each relevant rule or other thesis, did the writer provide enough information about each significant authority so that the reader was able to understand its relevance to the writer's analysis?

Does the writer avoid stretching the truth and avoid other inaccuracies when describing the law and the facts?

As needed, did the writer's argument make clear why the Court should accept the writer's arguments on each issue as opposed to the other side's arguments?

Within each section or sub-section of the argument, did the writer explicitly connect the case before the court to the rule, sub-rule, or other thesis? (i.e., did the writer apply the rule to the facts?)

Did the writer explicitly end the discussion of each issue and sub-issue by re-stating the conclusion the writer wants the court to reach on that issue and connecting that issue to the overall thesis as appropriate?

Did the writer make needed improvements from the macro draft?

Did the writer use headings, roadmaps, topic sentences, and connection-conclusions to signal organization to the reader, and did the writer connect every section and sub-section to the relevant point headings? Does the intro/roadmap material include legal backstory as appropriate? Does it cite to authority as needed?

FINAL COMMENT

To receive the best possible score in any area on the final draft, the writer should note the revision level suggested below.

A. CONTENT & ORGANIZATION (including research & presentation of issues)
COMMENTS:

___Significant revision needed ___throughout___as noted
___Moderate revision needed ___throughout ___ as noted
___Minimal revision needed ___throughout ___as noted
___Don't touch it

B. LEGAL ANALYSIS (including rule articulation, explanation (discussion of authority cases) and application of law to facts)
COMMENTS:

___Significant revision needed ___throughout___as noted
___Moderate revision needed ___throughout___ as noted
___Minimal revision needed ___throughout___as noted
___Don't touch it

C. WRITING STYLE (including small-scale organization & sentence structure)
COMMENTS:

___Significant revision needed ___throughout___as noted
___Moderate revision needed ___throughout ___ as noted
___Minimal revision needed ___throughout ___as noted
___Don't touch it

D. MECHANICS (including grammar, punctuation, & citation form)
COMMENTS:

___Significant revision needed ___throughout___as noted
___Moderate revision needed ___throughout ___ as noted
___Minimal revision needed ___throughout ___as noted
___Don't touch it

OTHER COMMENTS:

File your brief electronically by 9:00 p.m. on Sunday & turn in **3 hard copies** to room 255 by 8:00 a.m. on Monday. Attach this criteria sheet to one of the copies. You must also produce one copy for your opponent. Filing requirements for your opponent's copy will be posted on the course website and discussed in class. Make sure that your name is on <u>all copies</u> of the brief.

STUDENT:_____

FINAL DRAFT CRITERIA SHEET
APPELLATE ADVOCACY 600

I. Professionalism

A. Does the document include the following elements, formatted correctly? 1) Cover Sheet, 2) Question(s) Presented, 3) Parties to the Proceeding (if needed), 4) Table of Contents, 5) Table of Authorities, 6) Opinions Below, 7) Jurisdiction (with *appropriate* citation), 8) Constitutional and/or Statutory Provisions Involved (if needed), 9) Standard of Review, 10) Statement of the Case, 11) Summary of the Argument, 12) Argument, 13) Conclusion, 14) Signature Block, 15) Appendix (if needed), 16) Certificate of Service, 17) Certificate of Compliance with honor code certification. (See also Course materials, <u>APG</u> ch. 8 & Appendixes.)

B. <u>Question(s) Presented</u> (See <u>APG</u> ch. 9) Has the writer included appropriate question(s) presented? Does each question appropriately reflect the writer's theme? Does each question avoid assuming elements at issue and avoid other problems?

C. <u>Standard of Review</u> (See <u>APG</u> ch. 2) Does the writer identify the correct appellate standard of review? Does the writer cite appropriate authority for the standard?

D. <u>Statement of the Case</u> (See <u>APG</u> ch. 9) Does the Statement 1) begin with context, 2) include the procedural and factual history of the case, 3) include cites to the appendixes and/or record, 4) use persuasive techniques appropriately and effectively, and 5) include only honest and accurate information?

E. <u>Summary of the Argument</u> (See <u>APG</u> ch. 9) Does the summary provide a concise roadmap OR an argumentative overview of the argument, using case and statutory citations only as appropriate?

F. <u>Argument & Point Headings</u> (See <u>APG</u> ch. 5-9) Has the writer included an argument section that meets the criteria noted in Parts II-III below? Within the argument, are the Point Headings argumentative sentences that make specific points about the writer's argument, and do they divide the argument into appropriate CREXAC units of discourse?

G. <u>Conclusion/Signature Block</u> (See <u>APG</u> ch. 8) Has the writer explicitly told the court to grant the appropriate relief? (e.g., "this Court should affirm/reverse. . .") If more information is included, has the writer focused the conclusion? Did the writer sign the Certificate of Compliance and include other signature blocks as needed?

H. <u>Appendix</u> (See <u>APG</u> ch. 8) Has the writer included an appendix only if needed? If needed, does the appendix include appropriate legislation or other materials?

I. Is the document <u>double-spaced</u> and <u>paginated</u>? Were digital and hard copies turned in on time <u>with this sheet attached to the hard copy</u>? Are typographical errors corrected neatly in pen?

II. Research & Issue Identification

Did the writer identify all of the relevant legal issues and sub-issues within the Argument? Does the writer make all or most of the best arguments available?
Did the writer cite appropriate authority for each legal proposition?

Did the writer support the arguments made with all or most of the best authorities (i.e., applicable statutes, significant cases, etc.) relevant to each issue?

Did the writer avoid overstating the strength or weakness of the relevant authorities and facts?

If appropriate, has the writer gone beyond the authorities cited in the record to more recent authorities and/or to authorities more appropriate for a Supreme Court Brief?

Did the writer avoid irrelevant issues and arguments without valid support?

III. Argument: Organization & Legal Analysis

Did the writer organize the Argument around the identified issues and sub-issues, or organize the Argument in some other manner that allows the reader to understand easily how the authorities and arguments relate to the case? Did the writer address the strongest issue first or follow another logical method of ordering the issues (e.g., discussing a threshold issue first)?

Does the writer reconcile any seemingly inconsistent arguments?

Does each section or sub-section within the argument focus on an applicable rule, sub-rule, policy, or other thesis? Does the writer make clear how each point connects to the rule(s) that govern the case or to the brief's main thesis?

Did the writer adequately explain the significance of the rule or thesis that is the focus of each section? Unless circumstances dictated otherwise, did the writer finish explaining the rule *before* applying it to the facts?

When explaining each relevant rule or other thesis, did the writer provide enough information about each significant authority so that the reader was able to understand its relevance to the writer's analysis?

Does the writer avoid stretching the truth and avoid other inaccuracies when describing the law and the facts?

As needed, did the writer's argument make clear why the Court should accept the writer's arguments on each issue as opposed to the other side's arguments?

Within each section or sub-section of the argument, did the writer explicitly connect the case before the court to the rule, sub-rule, or other thesis? (i.e., did the writer apply the rule to the facts?)

Did the writer explicitly end the discussion of each issue and sub-issue by re-stating the conclusion the writer wants the court to reach on that issue and connecting that issue to the overall thesis as appropriate?

Did the writer make needed improvements from the micro draft?

Did the writer use headings, roadmaps, topic sentences, and connection-conclusions to signal organization to the reader, and did the writer connect every section and sub-section to the relevant point headings? Does the intro/roadmap material include legal backstory as appropriate? Does it cite to authority as needed?

V. Polishing (Max. = 0; Min. = -15)_____

A. Did the writer avoid errors caused by lack of proofreading?

B. Do all subjects agree with their verbs, and did the writer avoid other grammatical problems?
C. Did the writer use pronouns (especially "this," "they," and "it") precisely?

D. Did the writer use understandable sentence structures and avoid misplaced modifiers and parallelism problems?

E. Did the writer avoid sentence fragments and run-on sentences?

F. Is the document punctuated correctly?

G. Did the writer avoid spelling errors?

H. Did the writer avoid contractions, slang, and other uses of language inappropriate in an appellate brief?
I. Did the writer cite to authority when necessary?

J. Did the writer use correct citation form throughout?

K. Did the writer use short citation forms and citation sentences to incorporate citations to authority into the document as unobtrusively as possible?

****

Total points for this draft
      (out of 65)   _____

MINUS points taken off
on the MACRO DRAFT? _____

MINUS points taken off
on the MICRO draft?   _____

FINAL SCORE FOR
APPELLATE BRIEF   _____
(note that this is a _raw_ score)

Deductions for lateness will be taken from the course's final grade. Please record unexcused late days (or partial days) below.

_____Unexcused days late on Macro Draft

_____Unexcused days late on Micro Draft

_____Unexcused days late on Final Draft

_____   Electronic copies identical to hard copies?

Final Comment:

Fill in your name and then attach this sheet to the top of your ANNOTATED OUTLINE and turn both in together to my faculty mailbox on your due date.

STUDENT:_____

CRITERIA SHEET
ANNOTATED OUTLINE FOR MOTION BRIEF

(Max. = 0; Min. = -15)_____
[The final draft will be scored on a 65-point scale. Points deducted from this draft will be deducted from that 65 points.]

I.   MINIMUM REQUIREMENTS

A.   Does the outline include the following elements? 1) Standard of Review, 2) Working Headings, 3) Rule(s), 4) Support , 5) Leftovers (optional). Has the writer followed the guidelines for each of the sections?

B.   Is the document neatly typed and paginated, with adequate margins, and is this sheet attached with the student's name filled in?

II.   STANDARD OF REVIEW

Did the writer quote the correct standard of review for this motion and provide mandatory authority for the standard?

III.   WORKING HEADINGS

A.   In working headings and sub-headings, did the writer accurately identify all or most of the assertions that he or she wants to convince the court to agree with in order to prevail?

B.   Are the headings and sub-headings built around the issues and sub-issues that the case presents?

IV.   RULES

A.   Within each of the headings or sub-headings, did the writer accurately identify or formulate the relevant legal rules that could or would apply?

B.   Did the writer present the rules in a logical order?

V.   SUPPORT

A.   Within each heading or sub-heading, did the writer list all or most of the significant authorities that could be used to support, explain, or illustrate each rule?

B.   For each authority listed, did the writer include a short, accurate, description?

C.   Did the writer include citation information for each authority listed as support?

VI.   LEFTOVERS (Optional)

A.   Did the writer include rules and/or authorities that for some reason did not "fit" in the main outline?

B.   If the writer included extra authorities, did the writer include all information requested in Section V. above?

C.   Did the writer include private memo information explaining why the leftovers are included?

VII.   PRIVATE MEMO

Did the writer ask "private memo" questions, either separately or in footnotes?

VIII.   PROFESSIONALISM

A. Did the student fulfill class attendance requirements, including class preparation and participation?

B. Does the writing evidence good faith effort in fulfilling the requirements?

C. Did the student attend the scheduled conference and participate effectively in the conference?

D. Other

FINAL COMMENT:

Fill in your name and then staple this sheet to the top of your MACRO DRAFT and turn both in together to my faculty mailbox.

STUDENT:_____

CRITERIA SHEET
MOTION MEMO MACRO DRAFT

Score (Max. = 0; Min. = -15) _____   Dicta Grade: _____

I. MINIMUM REQUIREMENTS

A. Does the document include the required elements in order? 1) Caption & Title, 2) Introduction, 3) Argument, and 4) Conclusion?

B. Does the Introduction identify the specific legal issue that is before the court?

C. Are the Point Headings sentences that make specific points about the writer's argument, and are they used appropriately?

D. Within the Conclusion, has the writer specifically requested the desired relief?

E. Is the document neatly typed (**paginated**, double-spaced, and with adequate margins), and is this sheet attached with the student's name filled in? Did the student include private memos?

II. RESEARCH & ISSUE IDENTIFICATION

A. Did the writer accurately identify all of the major legal issues and ignore irrelevant issues?

B. Did the writer cite or cite and discuss the significant authorities relevant to each issue? Did the writer choose the best authorities available and ignore irrelevant authorities?

C. Did the writer include citations when needed?

III. ARGUMENT: ORGANIZATION & ANALYSIS

A. Is the argument organized around the rules and sub-rules or in some other logical way?

B. Did the writer begin the argument section, and any complex sub-sections within the argument section, with an "umbrella" section designed to:

   1) summarize the major rule or rules and explain how those rule(s) and the significant sub-rules relate to the issues and the ultimate conclusion;
   2) identify the relevant standard of review and cite to authority for that standard;
   3) explain the status of any relevant elements that will <u>not</u> be addressed;
   4) clarify, explicitly or implicitly, the order in which the remaining issues will be discussed; and
   5) assert the correctness of the ruling that the writer seeks?

C. At an appropriate place within each point heading section or subsection, did the writer state the rule and cite to authority for that rule? If statutory language is at issue, did the writer quote the relevant statutory language early in the argument?

III. ARGUMENT: ORGANIZATION & ANALYSIS (Cont'd)

D. Did the writer adequately explain each rule and sub-rule, e.g., by illustrating how that rule or sub-rule has been applied in the past and/or in other jurisdictions?

E. Even though the writer may have cited authorities from other jurisdictions, were those authorities always cited in the context of their relationship to mandatory rules?

F. When describing significant authority cases, did the writer include, at an appropriate level of detail, the relevant issue, disposition of issue (and of case, as appropriate), facts, and reasoning of the cases?

G. Did the writer address the other side of each issue as needed (either "offensively" or "defensively"), e.g., explaining why the client's arguments on the issues are valid and why the opponent's arguments are irrelevant or invalid?

H. Did the writer tie the arguments made to the relevant rules, using the language of the rule (i.e., the "phrases that pay") when applying the rule to the facts?

I. Even though the writer may be using persuasive techniques, is the law described honestly and accurately?

J. Did the writer explicitly end each point heading section with a connection-conclusion?

IV. PROFESSIONALISM

A. Did the student fulfill class attendance requirements, including class preparation and participation?

B. Does the writing evidence good faith effort in fulfilling the requirements?

C. Did the student prepare for the conference as needed, and was the student able to participate effectively in the conference?

D. Other

STUDENT:_____

FINAL COMMENT
No critique can or should identify every possible writing and/or analytical problem. To receive the best possible score in any area on the final draft, however, the writer should note the revision level suggested below when revising.

A. CONTENT & ORGANIZATION (including research & presentation of issues)
COMMENTS:
___Significant revision needed ___throughout___as noted
___Moderate revision needed ___throughout ___ as noted
___Minimal revision needed ___throughout ___as noted
___Don't touch it

B. LEGAL ANALYSIS (including rule articulation, explanation (discussion of authority cases) and application of law to facts)
COMMENTS:
___Significant revision needed ___throughout___as noted
___Moderate revision needed ___throughout___ as noted
___Minimal revision needed ___throughout___as noted
___Don't touch it

C. WRITING STYLE (including small-scale organization & sentence structure)
COMMENTS:
___Significant revision needed ___throughout___as noted
___Moderate revision needed ___throughout ___ as noted
___Minimal revision needed ___throughout ___as noted
___Don't touch it

D. MECHANICS (including grammar, punctuation, & citation form)
COMMENTS:
___Significant revision needed ___throughout___as noted
___Moderate revision needed ___throughout ___ as noted
___Minimal revision needed ___throughout ___as noted
___Don't touch it

OTHER COMMENTS:

Turn your paper in electronically by that deadline. Fill in your name,then staple this sheet to the top of your MICRO DRAFT and turn both in together as assigned.

STUDENT:_____

CRITERIA SHEET
MOTION MEMO MICRO DRAFT

Score (Max. = 0; Min. = -15)_____
> [The final draft of the motion memorandum will be scored on a 65-point scale. Points deducted from this draft will be deducted from that total.]

I. MINIMUM REQUIREMENTS

A. Does the document include the required elements **in order?** 1) Caption & Title, 2) Introduction, 3) Statute(s) Involved, 4) Statement of the Case, 5) Argument, 6) Conclusion, and 7) Certificate of Service?

B. Does the Introduction identify the specific legal issue that is before the court?

C. Does the Statement of the Case include the procedural history of the case, and appropriate citations to the record? Does it include the needed legally significant facts and relevant background facts? Does it use persuasive techniques appropriately and describe the facts honestly?

D. Are the Point Headings sentences that make specific points about the argument, and are they used appropriately?

E. Within the Conclusion, has the writer specifically requested the desired relief?

F. Is the document neatly typed (<u>paginated</u>, double-spaced, and with adequate margins), and is this sheet attached?

G. Did the writer include private memo notes seeking specific guidance and identifying strengths and weaknesses in the draft?

II. RESEARCH & ISSUE IDENTIFICATION

A. Did the writer accurately identify all of the major legal issues and ignore irrelevant issues?

B. Did the writer cite or cite and discuss the significant authorities relevant to each issue? Did the writer choose the best authorities available and ignore irrelevant authorities?

C. Did the writer include citations when needed?

III. ARGUMENT: ORGANIZATION & ANALYSIS

A. Is the argument organized around the rules and sub-rules or in some other logical way?

B. Did the writer begin the argument section, and any complex sub-sections within the argument section, with an introduction that includes "legal backstory" and a roadmap?

C. Within the backstory or roadmap, does the document do the following <u>if needed</u>? 1) Identify the question that it will ultimately answer, perhaps by stating the answer as a conclusion or an assertion. 2) Identify the legal standard at the root of the controversy. 3) Clarify how the current issue relates to that legal standard. 4) Clarify the current status of the issue in the relevant jurisdiction. 5) Identify the relevant standard of review and cite authority for that standard?

D. Does the introductory backstory/roadmap accomplish the following?
   1) summarize the major rule or rules and explain how those rule(s) and the significant sub-rules relate to the issues and the ultimate conclusion;
   2) explain the status of any relevant elements that will not be addressed, if any;
   3) clarify, explicitly or implicitly, the order in which the issues will be discussed; and
   4) assert the correctness of the ruling that the writer seeks?

E. Throughout, has the writer signaled the document's organization by suitable use of argumentative roadmap paragraphs, point headings, topic sentences, and signposts?

F. At an appropriate place within each point heading section or subsection, did the writer state the rule and cite to authority for that rule? If the rule comes from statutory language *or* is a gloss on statutory language, did the writer quote the relevant statutory language early in the section or subsection?

G. Did the writer adequately explain each rule and sub-rule, e.g., by illustrating how it has been applied?

H. If the writer cited authorities from other jurisdictions, were they cited in the context of their relationship to mandatory rules?

I. When describing significant authority cases, did the writer include, at an appropriate level of detail, the relevant issue, disposition of issue (and of case, as appropriate), facts, and reasoning of the cases?

J. Did the writer address the other side of each issue as needed (either "offensively" or "defensively"), e.g., by explaining why the client's arguments on the issues are valid and why the opponent's arguments are irrelevant or invalid?

K. Did the writer tie the arguments made to the relevant rules, using the language of the rule (i.e., the "phrases that pay") when applying the rule to the facts?

L. Do all or almost all of the paragraphs and paragraph blocks contain an argumentative topic sentence, and do the sentences within each paragraph or block relate to the thesis?

M. Even though the writer may be using persuasive techniques, is the law described honestly and accurately?

N. Did the writer explicitly end each point heading section with a connection-conclusion (i.e., a conclusion for the issue or sub-issue being discussed)?

IV. PROFESSIONALISM

A. Did the student fulfill class attendance requirements, including class preparation and participation?

B. Does the writing evidence good faith effort in fulfilling the requirements?

C. Was the student prepared for the conference?

FINAL COMMENT

No critique can identify every problem; to receive the best possible score in any area on the final draft, the writer should note the breadth and scope of revision suggested below.

A.   CONTENT & ORGANIZATION (including research & presentation of issues)
COMMENTS: ___Significant revision needed ___throughout___as noted
                                                                 ___Moderate revision needed ___throughout ___as noted
                                                                 ___Minimal revision needed ___throughout ___as noted
                                                                 ___Don't touch it

B.   LEGAL ANALYSIS (including use of the formula & case descriptions)
COMMENTS: ___Significant revision needed ___throughout ___as noted
                                                                 ___Moderate revision needed ___throughout ___as noted
                                                                 ___Minimal revision needed ___throughout ___as noted
                                                                 ___Don't touch it

C.   WRITING STYLE (including small-scale organization & sentence structure)
COMMENTS: ___Significant revision needed ___throughout ___as noted
                                                                 ___Moderate revision needed ___throughout ___as noted
                                                                 ___Minimal revision needed ___throughout ___as noted
                                                                 ___Don't touch it

D.   MECHANICS (including grammar, punctuation, & citation form)
COMMENTS: ___Significant revision needed ___throughout___as noted
                                                                 ___Moderate revision needed ___throughout ___as noted
                                                                 ___Minimal revision needed ___throughout ___as noted
                                                                 ___Don't touch it

OTHER COMMENTS:

Turn a digital copy of your paper in to the electronic drop box on the course website by the deadline. Fill in your name on this sheet and attach it to the top of your FINAL DRAFT. Turn in as assigned.

STUDENT:_____

CRITERIA SHEET
FINAL DRAFT – MOTION MEMO

I. MINIMUM REQUIREMENTS

A. Does the document include the required elements **in order?** 1) Caption & Title, 2) Introduction, 3) Statute(s) Involved, 4) Statement of the Case, 5) Argument, 6) Conclusion, and 7) Certificate of Service?

B. Does the Introduction identify the specific legal issue that is before the court?

C. Does the Statement of the Case include the procedural history of the case, and appropriate citations to the record? Does it include the needed legally significant facts and relevant background facts? Does it use persuasive techniques appropriately and describe the facts honestly?

D. Are the Point Headings sentences that make specific points about the argument, and are they used appropriately?

E. Within the Conclusion, has the writer specifically requested the desired relief?

F. Is the document neatly typed (paginated, double-spaced, and with adequate margins), and is this sheet attached?

G. Did the writer include private memo notes seeking specific guidance and identifying strengths and weaknesses in the draft?

II. RESEARCH & ISSUE IDENTIFICATION

A. Did the writer accurately identify all of the major legal issues and ignore irrelevant issues?

B. Did the writer cite or cite and discuss the significant authorities relevant to each issue? Did the writer choose the best authorities available and ignore irrelevant authorities?

C. Did the writer include citations when needed?

III. ARGUMENT: ORGANIZATION & ANALYSIS

A. Is the argument organized around the rules and sub-rules or in some other logical way?

B. Did the writer begin the argument section, and any complex sub-sections within the argument section, with an introduction that includes "legal backstory" and a roadmap?

C. Within the backstory or roadmap, does the document do the following if needed? 1) Identify the question that it will ultimately answer, perhaps by stating the answer as a conclusion or an assertion. 2) Identify the legal standard at the root of the controversy. 3) Clarify how the current issue relates to that legal standard. 4) Clarify the current status of the issue in the relevant jurisdiction. 5) Identify the relevant standard of review and cite authority for that standard?

D. Does the introductory backstory/roadmap accomplish the following?
   1) summarize the major rule or rules and explain how those rule(s) and the significant sub-rules relate to the issues and the ultimate conclusion;

2) explain the status of any relevant elements that will not be addressed, if any;

3) clarify, explicitly or implicitly, the order in which the issues will be discussed; and

4) assert the correctness of the ruling that the writer seeks?

E. Throughout, has the writer signaled the document's organization by suitable use of argumentative roadmap paragraphs, point headings, topic sentences, and signposts?

F. At an appropriate place within each point heading section or subsection, did the writer state the rule and cite to authority for that rule? If the rule comes from statutory language *or* is a gloss on statutory language, did the writer quote the relevant statutory language early in the section or subsection?

G. Did the writer adequately explain each rule and sub-rule, e.g., by illustrating how it has been applied?

H. If the writer cited authorities from other jurisdictions, were they cited in the context of their relationship to mandatory rules?

I. When describing significant authority cases, did the writer include, at an appropriate level of detail, the relevant issue, disposition of issue (and of case, as appropriate), facts, and reasoning of the cases?

J. Did the writer address the other side of each issue as needed (either "offensively" or "defensively"), e.g., by explaining why the client's arguments on the issues are valid and why the opponent's arguments are irrelevant or invalid?

K. Did the writer tie the arguments made to the relevant rules, using the language of the rule (i.e., the "phrases that pay") when applying the rule to the facts?

L. Do all or almost all of the paragraphs and paragraph blocks contain an argumentative topic sentence, and do the sentences within each paragraph or block relate to the thesis?

M. Even though the writer may be using persuasive techniques, is the law described honestly and accurately?

N. Did the writer explicitly end each point heading section with a connection-conclusion (i.e., a conclusion for the issue or sub-issue being discussed)?

IV. PROFESSIONALISM

A. Did the student fulfill class attendance requirements, including class preparation and participation?

B. Does the writing evidence good faith effort in fulfilling the requirements?

V. WRITING STYLE & MECHANICS
(Max. = 0; Min. = -20)

A. Do all subjects agree with their verbs, and did the writer use pronouns (especially "this" and "it") precisely?

B. Did the writer use understandable sentence structures and avoid misplaced modifiers and parallelism problems?

C. Did the writer use effective syntax and word choice and avoid wordiness, needless repetition, suspense, and other problems that interfere with reader comprehension?

D. Did the writer avoid sentence fragments and run-on sentences, as well as other grammatical errors?

E. Did the writer use verb tense appropriately?

F. Did the writer avoid overlong paragraphs and sentences?

G. Is the document punctuated correctly?

H. Did the writer avoid spelling errors?
I. Did the writer use citations when needed? Did the writer use correct citation form throughout?

J. Did the writer incorporate citations unobtrusively by using short citation forms and citation sentences whenever possible? Did the writer avoid including a long-form citation at the beginning of a sentence?

K. Did the writer avoid errors caused by lack of proofreading?

_____

TOTAL: (out of 65)   _____

MINUS points taken off
on the OUTLINE?   _____

MINUS points taken off
on the MICRO draft?   _____

FINAL SCORE FOR
OFFICE MEMO   _____
(Note that this is
a RAW score)   _____

Deductions for lateness will be taken from the final grade in the course. Unexcused late days are recorded below.

_____Unexcused days late on Macro draft

_____Unexcused days late on Micro draft

_____Unexcused days late on Final draft

FINAL COMMENT:

ORAL ARGUMENT CRITERIA

A.   Early in the argument, did counsel introduce the issue(s) to be discussed? Did counsel make his or her position on each issue evident?

B.   Did counsel present an outline of the argument organized to emphasize the case's best points?

C.   Did counsel demonstrate receptivity to questions by maintaining eye contact with the court and by listening when the court asked questions?

D.   Did counsel demonstrate knowledge of the case and its governing authorities in the following ways, as appropriate?

   1) Was counsel able to answer all or most of the reasonable questions from the bench?

   2) Did counsel support answers to questions with reference to legal authority or, when appropriate, the facts of the case?

   3) If appropriate, did counsel speak knowledgeably about the potential impact on future cases of the Court's possible holdings in this case?

   4) Did counsel avoid concessions unless a) the concession was necessary, and b) the concession did not undermine counsel's ultimate goal?

   5) Was counsel able to recognize friendly questions and respond to them appropriately?

E.   Did counsel respond professionally if unable to answer a question?

F.   Did counsel answer questions directly and provide a persuasive explanation for the answer?

G.   Did counsel move effectively between answering questions and argument?

H.   Did counsel request the appropriate relief, or was the requested relief apparent from the argument itself?

I.   Did counsel avoid reading and speak loudly enough to be understood?

J.   Did counsel appear to be poised and in control, and were counsel's grammar, diction, tone, and mannerisms appropriate?

K.   Was counsel respectful of the court and of his or her opponent before, during, and after the argument?

Score: _____/100

Sample Annotated Outline (with Sample "Private Memos")
Sarah Student

Standard of Review

The Minnesota Supreme Court erred as a matter of law when it reversed the trial court's decision. This Court accepts the trial court's findings of fact unless clearly erroneous, but decides questions of law de novo. United States v. United States Gypsum Co., 333 U.S. 364, 395 (1948).

Working Headings, Rules, and Support

I. Respondents are not protected under the Fourth Amendment because they had no legitimate expectation of privacy.

A. Respondents did not meet their burden of proof in establishing that they had a legitimate expectation of privacy.

Rules:

Only individuals who demonstrate a legitimate expectation of privacy can claim the protection of the Fourth Amendment. Before a criminal defendant can bring a motion to suppress evidence on the basis that it was obtained in violation of the Fourth Amendment, the defendant has the burden of proof that he is a proper party to assert the claim of illegality and to seek the remedy of exclusion.

Support:

The Fourth Amendment to the United States Constitution
The 4th amendment guarantees "[t]he right of the people to be secure in their persons, houses, papers, and effects, against unreasonable searches and seizures." U.S. Const. Amend. IV.[3]

Rakas v. Illinois, 439 U.S. 128, 130-31 (1978)
Motion to suppress denied where defendants were passengers in car that was searched because they had no legitimate expectation of privacy in car they didn't own.

Jones v. United States, 362 U.S. 257 (1960)
Court found that "it is entirely proper to require of one who seeks to challenge the legality of a search as the basis for suppressing relevant evidence that he allege, and if the allegation be disputed, that he establish, that he himself was a victim of an invasion of privacy." Court held that person had to establish that he was "legitimately on the premises" to have standing to challenge the legality of a search.

---

[3]I presume that I need to start with the fourth amendment. Do I put it in between the "I" and the "A"? Or should I put it even before the "I"?

B. Respondents had no legitimate expectation of privacy because any subjective expectation they might have had while temporarily in another's home for the sole purpose of conducting illegal business was not one society recognizes as reasonable.

1. The <u>Olson</u> rule dictates that only overnight guests have a connection to a premises that gives rise to a legitimate expectation of privacy.

Rule:

"[S]tatus as an overnight guest is alone enough to show that [the defendant] had an expectation of privacy in the home that society is prepared to recognize as reasonable."

Support:

<u>Minnesota v. Olson</u>, 495 U.S. 91 (1990)
Apartment guest had a reasonable expectation of privacy and was allowed to claim fourth amendment protection in friend's apartment because he was an overnight guest and it's reasonable for an overnight guest to expect privacy because it serves functions recognized as valuable by society.

<u>Terry v. Martin</u>, 120 F.3d 661, 664 (7th Cir. 1997)
Held that the legitimate expectation of privacy realized by overnight guests did not extend to confer Fourth Amendment standing on temporary visitors present in an apartment for the purpose of buying heroin.

<u>United States v. Hicks</u>, 978 F.2d 722, 724 (D.C. Cir. 1992)
Held that a guest who used an apartment to distribute cocaine had no legitimate expectation of privacy.

<u>State v. Wise</u>, 879 S. W.2d 494, 505 (Mo. 1994)
Held that a defendant who was in an apartment to use the telephone had no legitimate expectation of privacy.

<u>Villarreal v. State</u>, 893 S.W.2d 559, 561 (Texas Ct. App. 1994)
Court declined to extend the <u>Olson</u> expectation to an invited guest who had not stayed overnight but "was welcome to stay if he wanted to."

<u>Lewis v. United States</u>, 594 A.2d 542, 546 (D.C. 1991).
The court held that a party guest who happened to fall asleep for several hours in a bedroom could not assert a Fourth Amendment challenge to a search of the apartment. The court ruled that because Lewis offered no evidence that he had been invited to spend the night or intended to do so, he had not shown a legitimate expectation of privacy. The court reasoned that a mere guest who is not spending the night is substantially different from the overnight guest who receives standing under <u>Olson</u>.

2. Even if the <u>Olson</u> rule extends to non-overnight guests, Respondents' expectation of privacy is unreasonable because they were present only to conduct illegal business that is not valuable to society.

Rule:

Only those non-overnight guests whose connections to the home give rise to an expectation of privacy that society is prepared to recognize as reasonable can bring a fourth amendment challenge.

Support:

Minnesota v. Olson, 495 U.S. 91 (1990)
Apartment guest had a reasonable expectation of privacy and was allowed to claim fourth amendment protection in friend's apartment because he was an overnight guest and it's reasonable for an overnight guest to expect privacy because it serves functions recognized as valuable by society.

Rakas v. Illinois, 439 U.S. 128, 130-31 (1978)
Motion to suppress denied where defendants were passengers in car that was searched because they had no legitimate expectation of privacy in car they didn't own. n.12: a legitimate expectation is one that is rooted in "understandings that are recognized and permitted by society."

People v. Moreno, 3 Cal. Rptr. 2d 66, 70 (Cal. Ct. App. 1992)
California court found that a defendant who moved to suppress items seized at his brother's apartment while the defendant was babysitting there had a legitimate expectation of privacy and could challenge fruits of search. Court cited Olson and indicated that, "[l]ike 'staying overnight in another's home,' babysitting 'is a longstanding social custom that serves functions recognized as valuable by society.'"

Junior v. United States, 634 A.2d 411, 419 (D.C. 1993).
Defendant who regularly visited a home to feed and care for the homeowner's retarded adult son had a legitimate expectation of privacy "rooted in understandings that are recognized and permitted by society."

Treasury Employees v. Von Raab, 489 U.S. 656, 668, 674 (1989).
Court allowed drug testing of certain treasury employees, noting that possession, use, and distribution of illegal drugs represent "one of the greatest problems affecting the health and welfare of our population" and thus "one of the most serious problems confronting our society today."

Employment Div., Dept. of Human Resources of Oregon v. Smith, 494 U.S. 872 (1990)
The free exercise clause of the First Amendment does not prohibit application of Oregon drug laws to the ceremonial ingestion of peyote.

Lewis v. United States, 385 U.S. 206, 211 (1966).
A defendant who used his home for the felonious sale of narcotics could not claim a violation of any reasonable expectation of privacy when an undercover officer entered the home to purchase marijuana.

United States v. Hicks, 978 F.2d 722 (D.C. Cir. 1992).
A visitor who used another's apartment solely to conduct drug transactions could not claim Fourth Amendment protection. The court reasoned that the defendant "treated the apartment as a base for his business operation, not as a sanctuary from outsiders." "Hicks was not engaging in any longstanding social custom that serves functions recognized as valuable by society."[4]

C. Respondents may not claim a legitimate expectation of privacy, because by engaging in criminal

---

[4]I know we're not supposed to use too many non-supreme court cases, but I think the various facts of these cases help make my point. I'm going to do my best to tie them to the rule from the Supreme Court case, in this section and other sections. Some of the cases I got by shepardizing the Supreme Court case, so that will help!

acts in a well-lit room, directly in front of a window facing a widely-used common area, they exhibited no subjective expectation of privacy.

Rule:

An individual seeking to establish that he possessed a legitimate expectation of privacy must first demonstrate that he possessed an "actual (subjective) expectation of privacy."

Support:

Katz v. United States, 389 U.S. 347, 361 (Harlan, J., concurring).
The defendant exhibited a subjective expectation of privacy when he closed the door to a telephone booth to prevent being overheard. Katz did not knowingly expose his activity to the public; rather, his conduct demonstrated his intent to keep the activity private. Therefore, the government "violated the privacy upon which he justifiably relied" when it attached an electronic surveillance device to the telephone booth. "What a person knowingly exposes to the public, even in his own home or office, is not the subject of Fourth Amendment protections." Id. at 351.[5]

Smith v. Maryland, 442 U.S. 735 (1979).
Defendant who challenged the government's installation of a pen register to record his telephone calls had no actual, subjective expectation of privacy in phone numbers he dialed, because all telephone users realize that they must convey phone numbers to the telephone company and that the telephone company records the information.

California v. Ciraolo, 476 U.S. 207 (1985).
Defendant's motion to suppress properly denied because defendant who hid his marijuana crop from the public view with two fences may have "manifested merely a hope that no one would observe his unlawful gardening pursuits" and not an actual, subjective expectation of privacy.

D. This Court should maintain its reluctance to expand the class of individuals who may claim a legitimate expectation of privacy and invoke the exclusionary rule.

Rule/Thesis:

This Court should not expand the exclusionary rule because each application of the exclusionary rule "exacts a substantial social cost," as "[r]elevant and reliable evidence is kept from the trier of fact and the search for truth at trial is deflected."

Support:
Rakas v. Illinois, 439 U.S. 128, 130-31 (1978)
Motion to suppress denied where defendants were passengers in car that was searched because they had no legitimate expectation of privacy in car they didn't own. Court said that "misgivings as to the benefit of enlarging the class of persons who may invoke that rule are properly considered when deciding whether to expand standing to assert Fourth Amendment violations."

---

[5] I'm using Katz again to point out that Katz did *not* expose his behavior to the public but that the respondents *did.* The thumbs-up, thumbs-down PTP stuff. This is my case showing when a rule will *not* be applied to certain facts.

<u>Alderman v. United States</u>, 394 U.S. 165, 175 (1969)
Court held that defendants can argue for suppression of the product of a Fourth Amendment violation only if those defendants' rights were violated by the search itself. Codefendants and coconspirators have no special standing and cannot prevent admission against them of information which has been obtained through electronic surveillance which is illegal against another. Because of the potential harm, this Court has expressly ruled that only individuals whose rights were infringed by the search itself may urge suppression of the fruits of a Fourth Amendment violation. The additional benefits of extending the exclusionary rule to other defendants would not "justify further encroachment upon the public interest in prosecuting those accused of crime and having them acquitted or convicted on the basis of all the evidence which exposes the truth."

<u>United States v. Salvucci</u>, 448 U.S. 83 (1980).
Defendants couldn't claim right of privacy in apartment of the mother of one of them, so had no standing to claim exclusionary rule's protection to suppress evidence found in search of that apartment. To allow otherwise, the Court said, "serves only to afford a windfall to defendants whose Fourth Amendment rights have not been violated," an outcome that cannot be tolerated in light of the significant public interests in curbing crime and in fairly and accurately determining defendants' guilt or innocence at trial.

II. Officer Thielen's conduct was not a Fourth Amendment search because he stood in a location where any member of the public might have stood and observed the criminal activity in a manner any member of the public might have employed.

        A. No Fourth Amendment search occurred because the officer merely viewed what was in plain view from a publicly accessible common area outside the apartment's curtilage, where Respondents had no reasonable expectation of privacy.

Rule:
A person possesses a reasonable expectation of privacy, and thus, a search occurs, when an officer makes an observation from a location within the curtilage of a private home.

Support:
<u>California v. Ciraolo</u>, 476 U.S. 207, 212 (1986).
Defendant's marijuana in a 15-by-25 foot plot in his backyard searchable by plane despite 6-foot outer fence and 10-foot inner fence. Officers who flew over the defendant's house in a private airplane and readily identified the illegal plants using only the naked eye did not conduct a Fourth Amendment search because the airspace was outside the curtilage of the apartment, and the scene would have been in plain view to any member of the public flying in the same airspace.

<u>Oliver v. United States</u>, 466 U.S. 170, 180 (1984)
Officers who looked through fences on open fields and found marijuana plants did not violate fourth amendment. Court held open fields do *not* have the protection of lands associated with the home. Curtilage, "the land immediately surrounding and associated with the home," is "the area to which extends the intimate activity associated with the 'sanctity of a man's home and the privacies of life.'" <u>Id.</u>

<u>United States v. Dunn</u>, 480 U.S. 295, 301 (1987).
No 4th amendment violation when officers observed a drug laboratory inside the defendant's barn while standing outside the curtilage. <u>Id.</u> at 304. This Court held that even if the barn itself had been within the curtilage, the defendant could claim no reasonable expectation of privacy, because the scene was plainly visible from outside the curtilage. (Lays out 4-part curtilage test)

The primary focus of the curtilage test is whether the area "harbors those intimate activities associated with domestic life and the privacies of home." Id. at 304.

Martin v. United States, 183 F.2d 436, 439 (4th Cir. 1950)
Courts have ruled that curtilage can include garages,

Rozencranz v. United States, 356 F.2d 310, 313 (1st Cir. 1966),
barns,

Roberson v. United States, 165 F.2d 752, 754 (6th Cir. 1948),
smokehouses,

Florida v. Riley, 488 U.S. 445, 452 (1989) (plurality opinion),
greenhouses

United States v. Acevedo, 627 F.2d 68, 69 n.1 (7th Cir. 1980).
Aa surveillance officer's observation of an undercover heroin purchase while standing in a gangway to the side of an apartment complex did not violate expectation of privacy.

1 Wayne R. LaFave, Search and Seizure § 2.3(f) at 414 (2d ed. 1987).
The privacy expectation in apartment common areas "is often diminished because it is not subject to the exclusive control of one tenant and is utilized by tenants generally and numerous visitors attracted to a multiple occupancy building."

United States v. Holland, 755 F.2d 253, 255 (2d Cir. 1985)
Individual tenants in multi-tenant buildings have no legitimate expectation of privacy in common hallway areas, even when guarded by locked doors.

State v. Hines, 323 S.2d 449, 450 (La. 1975)
Apartment tenants have no reasonable expectation of privacy as to the "common yard open to the public."

United States v. Fields, 113 F.3d 313 (2d Cir. 1997)
A police officer's observation of defendants cooking and bagging crack cocaine through a partially covered first-floor apartment window was not a Fourth Amendment search, and distinguishing the case from cases involving single-family dwellings.

B. No Fourth Amendment search occurred because Officer Thielen, who used only his natural senses to observe the apartment without physical intrusion, took no extraordinary measures.

Rule:
No reasonable expectation of privacy exists when an officer takes only ordinary measures, using only his natural senses, to view what any private passerby could have viewed with no physical intrusion. This Court has repeatedly suggested that an officer does not take extraordinary measures when he simply observes an area without physically invading it.

Support:

California v. Ciraolo, 476 U.S. 207, 213-14 (1985).
Officers did not violate fourth amendment when they observed marijuana growing in defendant's backyard by flying over land in private plane. Court noted that members of public could be in same airspace and see what the officers saw.

1 Wayne R. LaFave, Search and Seizure § 2.3(f), at 414 (2d ed. 1987).
When the police "resort to the extraordinary step of positioning themselves where neither neighbors nor the general public would be expected to be, the observation or overhearing of what is occurring within a dwelling constitutes a Fourth Amendment search."

Texas v. Brown, 460 U.S. 730, 749 (1983).
An officer on a traffic stop who bent down at an angle so that he could see the inside of the defendant's car did not violate the fourth amendment because a member of the public could have done and seen the same things. court found no extraordinary measures taken.

State v. Smith, 181 A.2d 761 (N.J. 1962).
The warrantless arrest, search, and seizure of evidence were proper where the police observed criminal drug activity from a common passageway through a hole in a door molding and demanding admission would have benefitted those engaged in the activity. "Peering through a window or a crack in a door or a keyhole is not, in the abstract, genteel behavior, but the Fourth Amendment does not protect against all conduct unworthy of a good neighbor." Police have a duty to investigate, and "in striking a balance between the rights of the individual and the needs of law enforcement," the Fourth Amendment does not protect individuals from observations that impolite neighbors might have made.

Florida v. Riley, 488 U.S. 445, 449 (1989) (plurality opinion)
The Court held that there was no search when police observed marijuana in a defendant's greenhouse from a helicopter circling above the greenhouse. The Court emphasized that there was no evidence that the helicopter interfered with the normal use of the greenhouse, that intimate details connected with the use of the home were observed or that there was undue noise or threat of injury. Id. at 452. Because there was no physical invasion, the Court reasoned, the officers violated no reasonable expectation of privacy. Id.

Katz v. United States, 389 U.S. 347, 361 (Harlan, J., concurring).
Fourth amendment violation when government "violated the privacy upon which he justifiably relied" when it attached an electronic surveillance device to the telephone booth. Court indicated that the reach of the Fourth Amendment cannot turn on the presence or absence of a physical intrusion into an enclosure, but government in that case did not use natural senses.

Below are materials for a citation form worksheet. Because both the ALWD Manual and the Bluebook result in identical citations for purposes of this worksheet, the problems and the answer key are the same. The only difference is the attachment, which lists the relevant rules. If you use the ALWD manual, you should include the ALWD rules in your attachment; if you use the Bluebook manual, substitute the Bluebook rules for the ALWD rules. If you use both manuals, or allow students to use either of the two, you can give them both sets of rules.

CITATION FORM WORKSHEET

Read the instructions carefully before you begin. **Name:** _____

Please answer the questions on this worksheet IN PENCIL, and bring the completed worksheet to our next class meeting. You must have a completed worksheet to come into the class and to be counted as present for that day. You may complete the worksheet with a classmate, as long as each of you works on each question (that is, do not divide up the work). Indicate spaces within abbreviations by using ^ or some obvious symbol. **Assume that all citations will appear in an office memorandum as part of a citation sentence unless the question informs you differently.** For guidance, consult the rules at the end of the handout. The information for some of the citations is fictional; you should make up any page numbers needed or any other information that is missing. Please bring your citation guide to class.

1.   **Write the long form citation**: Raymond Hayes v. City of Chicago, Fred Rice, and Joseph Beazley, No. 87 C 0956, United States District Court for the Northern District of Illinois, Eastern Division, 710 F. Supp. 239; 1989 U.S. Dist. LEXIS 3888, Decided April 7, 1989.

2.   **(a)Write the long form citation; (b) write the short form (not Id.) citation**: 549 U.S. 1073; 127 S. Ct. 272; 166 L. Ed. 2d 209; 2006 U.S. LEXIS 6225, *; 75 U.S.L.W. 3172. Jeremiah E. Bulson, Petitioner v. State of Iowa//No. 06-5512.//SUPREME COURT OF THE UNITED STATES//549 U.S. 1073; 127 S. Ct. 272; 166 L. Ed. 2d 209; 2006 U.S. LEXIS 6225; 75 U.S.L.W. 3172

3.   **Write a short form citation to a case that cites another case.** Assume that you are citing to the following sentence from the Bulson case (from #2 above): "We find that Mr. Bulson did not have the 'intent to injure another' that is a needed element of the crime here." Assume that the phrase "intent to injure another" came from the following case: Illinois v. Marat, 111 U.S. 245 (1984). Write an appropriate short form citation to the Bulson case.

4.   **(a) Write the long form citation; (b) write the Id. form citation**: 18 So.3d 46, 34 Fla. L. Weekly D1853 District Court of Appeal of Florida, First District. Paul LENNON, Appellant, v. State of Florida, Appellee. No. 1D09-0697. Sept. 10, 2009. Assume that both citations appear in the dissenting opinion of Judge Nickels.

5.   **(a) Write the long form citation;(b) write the short form citation**: Section 9-30-5-18 of the Indiana Code. The statute was enacted in 1925, and a sentence was added to it in 2005. The date of the volume of The Burns Indiana Statutes Annotated (which you are using) is 2009; the date on the pocket part is 2010. You are citing the section in its entirety. Most of the statute is in the main volume; only the added sentence is in the pocket part. You may assume that you are citing the statute in a citation, not at the beginning of a textual sentence.

6.   (a) Re-write the citation that you wrote in answer to 4(a), with the signal that would be appropriate to use to indicate that the cited authority contains a legal proposition that you paraphrased. (b) Re-write the citation you wrote in answer to 2(b), with the signal that would be appropriate to use to indicate that the cited authority implies rather than states directly the point you are citing it for.

7.	Assume that the excerpt below is from an office memo, and that the indented material (beginning "The trial court sustained") is a quotation from page 1085 of the case cited in #2 above. Write an appropriate "Id. at" citation and put it in the appropriate place in relation to the quoted language.

The court specifically discussed the importance of objections:

> The trial court sustained the state's objection to Martin's testimony on the grounds that the primary purpose of calling Martin would be to impeach him by introducing evidence of prior inconsistent statements. The jury found Bulson guilty as to all five counts and he appealed his convictions. The state appellate court considered the exclusion of Martin's testimony, but summarily affirmed Martin's convictions.

8.	Write out a formal citation to the United States Constitution, Fourth Amendment.

9.	Read the paragraph on the next page. For each sentence in the paragraph, decide what citation (if any) is needed, and write either the citation or "no cite needed" after the corresponding number after the paragraph. (I have numbered the end of each sentence.) Assume that the "Adam Dante" case is the source for the first legal proposition and that the "Gary Corbin" case is the source for the second legal proposition. The source of later propositions should be evident in the text. Assume that neither case has been cited within the document before this paragraph. Both cases are from the highest court in Texas. You should make up page numbers for any pinpoint cites needed.

1) 483 S.W.2d 452, Supreme Court of Texas. ADAM DANTE CORPORATION d/b/a Adam and Eve Health Spa, Petitioner, v. Beulah H. SHARPE, Respondent. No. B-2859. June 21, 1972. Rehearing Denied July 26, 1972.

2) 648 S.W.2d 292, Supreme Court of Texas. Gary CORBIN, Petitioner, v. SAFEWAY STORES, INC., Respondent. No. C-1637. April 6, 1983.

The second means by which a landowner such as our client, ALC, can relieve itself of duty and liability toward invitees is to make the latent defect "safe."(1) A landowner makes a latent defect safe when he or she takes whatever action is "reasonably prudent" under the circumstances to reduce or eliminate the risk from the dangerous condition.(2) In Corbin, a man was injured when he slipped on a grape in the produce department when the usual non-slip mat was missing from the floor.(3) The court stated that additional measures such as bagging the grapes, giving warnings, or conducting frequent inspections would have been reasonably prudent to minimize risk and make the dangerous condition "safe."(4) In <u>Adam Dante</u>, where a health club patron sued after slipping on a foamy substance that lay under water that had overflowed from a whirlpool, the court stated that a health club owner should have made the latent defect "safe" by placing rubber mats on the floor to protect patrons from slipping and falling.(5) In this case, ALC, like the defendants in <u>Adam Dante</u> and <u>Corbin</u>, took no further actions to try to be reasonably prudent under the circumstances and reduce or eliminate the risk to invitees.(6) ALC did not enforce the restricted access to the renovation area and did not set up barricades around the area where the work was taking place.(7) Because ALC did not take reasonably prudent action to make latent defects safe, a court would probably hold that ALC breached the duty it owed to Mr. Krisher.(8)

1.

2.

3.

4.

5.

6.

7.

8.

Selected ALWD Rules:

Category:	ALWD Rule
Altering quotations	48, 49
Case citing another case	47.7
Case names	12.2
Constitutions	13.2
Court (in case cites)	12.6
Date (in case cites)	12.7
Id. & Case Short Form	11.3, 12.20
Lexis or Westlaw cites	12.12
Long quotes	47.5
Pinpoint Citations	5.2, 12.5
Public Domain Citations	
Reporters (in case cites)	12.3, 12.4
Sections and Paragraphs	6
Signal Words	44
Spacing & Abbreviations	2
Statutes	14
Subsequent History	12.8, 12.10
Typeface Conventions	1
Websites	40
Weight of Authority	12.11
When to cite	43.2

Selected Bluebook Rules:

Category	BB Rule
Altering quotations	5.2, 5.3
Case citing another case	10.6.2
Case names	B5.1.1, 10.2
Constitutions	B7, 11
Court (case cites)	B.5.1.3, 10.4
Date (case cites)	B.5.1.3, 10.5
Id. & Short Form	B5.2, 4.1, 10.9
Lexis or Westlaw cites	18.1
Long quotes	B12; 5.1
Pinpoint Citations	B.5.1.2,. 3.2
Public Domain Citations	10.3.3
Reporters (case cites)	B5.1.2, 10.3.1
Sections & Paragraphs	3.3, 6.2(c)
Signal Words	B4, 1.2

1. **Write the long form citation**: Raymond Hayes v. City of Chicago, Fred Rice, and Joseph Beazley, No. 87 C 0956, United States District Court for the Northern District of Illinois, Eastern Division, 710 F. Supp. 239; 1989 U.S. Dist. LEXIS 3888, Decided April 7, 1989.

Hayes^ v.^City^of^Chicago,^710^F.^Supp.^239,^245^(N.D.^Ill.^1989).

2. **(a)Write the long form citation; (b) write the short form (not Id.) citation**: 549 U.S. 1073; 127 S. Ct. 272; 166 L. Ed. 2d 209; 2006 U.S. LEXIS 6225, *; 75 U.S.L.W. 3172. Jeremiah E. Bulson, Petitioner v. State of Iowa//No. 06-5512.//SUPREME COURT OF THE UNITED STATES//549 U.S. 1073; 127 S. Ct. 272; 166 L. Ed. 2d 209; 2006 U.S. LEXIS 6225; 75 U.S.L.W. 3172

a.   Bulson^v.^Iowa,^549^U.S.^1073,^1090^(2006).

b.   Bulson,^549^U.S.^at^1092.

3. **Write a short form citation to a case that cites another case.** Assume that you are citing to the following sentence from the Bulson case (from #2 above): "We find that Mr. Bulson did not have the 'intent to injure another' that is a needed element of the crime here." Assume that the phrase "intent to injure another" came from the following case: Illinois v. Marat, 111 U.S. 245 (1984). Write an appropriate short form citation to the Bulson case.

Bulson,^549^U.S.^at^1092^(quoting^Illinois^v.^Marat,^111^U.S.^245,^255^(1984)).

4. **(a) Write the long form citation; (b) write the Id. form citation**: 18 So.3d 46, 34 Fla. L. Weekly D1853 District Court of Appeal of Florida, First District. Paul LENNON, Appellant, v. State of Florida, Appellee. No. 1D09-0697. Sept. 10, 2009. Assume that both citations appear in the dissenting opinion of Judge Nickels.

a.   Lennon v. State,^18^So.^3d^46,^66^(Fla.^1st^Dist.^App.^2009)^(Nickels,^J.,^dissenting).

b.   Id.^at^67^(Nickels,^J.,^dissenting).

5. **(a) Write the long form citation;(b) write the short form citation**: Section 9-30-5-18 of the Indiana Code. The statute was enacted in 1925, and a sentence was added to it in 2005. The date of the volume of The Burns Indiana Statutes Annotated (which you are using) is 2009; the date on the pocket part is 2010. You are citing the section in its entirety. Most of the statute is in the main volume; only the added sentence is in the pocket part. You may assume that you are citing the statute in a citation, not at the beginning of a textual sentence.

a.   Ind.^Code^Ann.^§^9-30-5-18^(LexisNexis^2009^&^Supp.^2010).

b.　§^9-30-5-18

6.　(a) Re-write the citation that you wrote in answer to 4(a), with the signal that would be appropriate to use to indicate that the cited authority contains a legal proposition that you paraphrased. (b) Re-write the citation you wrote in answer to 2(b), with the signal that would be appropriate to use to indicate that the cited authority implies rather than states directly the point you are citing it for.

　a. <u>Lennon v. State</u>,^18^So.^3d^46,^66^(Fla.^1st^Dist.^App.^2009)^(Nickels,^J.,^dissenting).

　b. <u>See^id.</u>^at^67^(Nickels,^J.,^dissenting).

7.　Assume that the excerpt below is from an office memo, and that the indented material (beginning "The trial court sustained") is a quotation from page 1085 of the case cited in #2 above. Write an appropriate "<u>Id.</u> at" citation and put it in the appropriate place in relation to the quoted language.

The court specifically discussed the importance of objections:

> The trial court sustained the state's objection to Martin's testimony on the grounds that the primary purpose of calling Martin would be to impeach him by introducing evidence of prior inconsistent statements. The jury found Bulson guilty as to all five counts and he appealed his convictions. The state appellate court considered the exclusion of Martin's testimony, but summarily affirmed Martin's convictions.

<u>Id.</u>^at^1085.

8.　Write out a formal citation to the United States Constitution, Fourth Amendment.

U.S.^Const.^amend.^IV.

9.　Read the paragraph below. For each sentence, decide what citation (if any) is needed, and write either the citation or "no cite needed" after the corresponding number after the paragraph. (I have numbered the end of each sentence.) Assume that the "Adam Dante" case is the source for the first legal proposition and that the "Gary Corbin" case is the source for the second legal proposition. The source of later propositions should be evident in the text. Assume that neither case has been cited within the document before this paragraph. Both cases are from the highest court in Texas. You should make up page numbers for any pinpoint cites needed.

1) 483 S.W.2d 452, Supreme Court of Texas. ADAM DANTE CORPORATION d/b/a Adam and Eve Health Spa, Petitioner, v. Beulah H. SHARPE, Respondent. No. B-2859. June 21, 1972. Rehearing Denied July 26, 1972.

2) 648 S.W.2d 292, Supreme Court of Texas. Gary CORBIN, Petitioner, v. SAFEWAY STORES,

INC., Respondent. No. C-1637. April 6, 1983.

The second means by which a landowner such as our client, ALC, can relieve itself of duty and liability toward invitees is to make the latent defect "safe."(1) A landowner makes a latent defect safe when he or she takes whatever action is "reasonably prudent" under the circumstances to reduce or eliminate the risk from the dangerous condition.(2) In Corbin, a man was injured when he slipped on a grape in the produce department when the usual non-slip mat was missing from the floor.(3) The court stated that additional measures such as bagging the grapes, giving warnings, or conducting frequent inspections would have been reasonably prudent to minimize risk and make the dangerous condition "safe."(4) In Adam Dante, where a health club patron sued after slipping on a foamy substance that lay under water that had overflowed from a whirlpool, the court stated that a health club owner should have made the latent defect "safe" by placing rubber mats on the floor to protect patrons from slipping and falling.(5) In this case, ALC, like the defendants in Adam Dante and Corbin, took no further actions to try to be reasonably prudent under the circumstances and reduce or eliminate the risk to invitees.(6) ALC did not enforce the restricted access to the renovation area and did not set up barricades around the area where the work was taking place.(7) Because ALC did not take reasonably prudent action to make latent defects safe, a court would probably find that ALC breached the duty it owed to Mr. Krisher.(8)

1. Adam^Dante^Corp.^v.^Sharpe,^483^S.W.2d^452,^452^(Tex.^1972).

2. Corbin^v.^Safeway^Stores,^Inc.,^648^S.W.2d^292,^299^(Tex.^1983).

3. 648^S.W.2d^at^295.^[OR Id.^at^295.]

4. Id.^at^302.

5. 483^S.W.2d^at^462. [OR: Adam^Dante^Corp.,^483^S.W.2d^at^462.]

6. [no cite needed]
7. [no cite needed]
8. [no cite needed]

Chapter One
Introduction

Possible Teaser(s) for Syllabus:
We will discuss what it means for an appellate advocate to "be the sun."
[*See* Section 1.4]

Learning Goals of Class Meeting:

Communicate the need for effective brief-writing based on the needs of the audience for the brief.

Communicate course requirements, including due dates, late paper policies, plagiarism and other honor code rules, and other expectations.

Communicate the method that will be used to write the documents, i.e., writing process methodology, number of drafts, etc.

Introduce concepts of writing process theory.

Acquaint students in a general way with what the final product looks like.

Distribute assignment.

Changes from Second Edition:

A brief discussion of writing theory has been added, focusing on the cognitivist and social perspective. These concepts can be helpful throughout the semester.

Items on Website:

[Note: To access the materials on the website (which are located under the Professor Materials tab), you will need to obtain a password by calling an Aspen Publishers sales assistant at 1-800-950-5259 or by emailing legaledu@wolterskluwer.com.]

Powerpoint of "readers" contains pictures of ideal and less ideal readers (described below). It also includes a quote from the 6th Harry Potter book that describes how many legal readers read, at least when they are tired.

Ideas for Lecture and Discussion:

You can assign the first chapter the first week of the semester. It is usually helpful to lay out the logistics of the semester and solicit questions so that you and the students are on the same page. If you use the "macro, micro, final" draft method, make sure that students understand what type of document will be required of them at each stage of the process. The powerpoint available on the website contains some slides defining these terms. You may wish to talk about the drafts as part of a general discussion of the writing process. As noted, the third edition contains some discussion of writing theory; the powerpoint defines some of the concepts relevant to writing theory, in particular with regard to the cognitive and social perspective schools.

I find that this discussion is most helpful when it occurs in the context of a discussion of audience. That is, rather than start with how the semester will work, I start by talking about their readers, and the needs of their readers, and then move to a discussion about how our work over the semester will teach them how to write a helpful document.

I find that students have a hard time grasping the reality of how people read; they believe that while they themselves may sometimes be careless or inattentive while reading, the people who read their work are "*uber*-readers" who pay careful attention at all times, who re-read anything they don't understand, and who may leave the text to look up missing information *and then return to the text.* I tell students that lawyers are too idealistic about their readers and that they need to be more cynical, and then I show them a series of pictures of readers, from those envisioned by idealists to those envisioned by cynics. These pictures are on the powerpoint on the book's website. Usually I can see wide-eyed reactions from at least some students every year, as they realize that their work as an attorney will be read by a *reader,* not by a *teacher.*

If your class is smaller, you may wish to engage them in a discussion about what they do when they read, and what they presume judges and clerks do when they read briefs from attorneys. If you discuss the fable of the sun and the wind, you may wish to point out how "being the sun" can include credibility and other intangibles of reputation as well as persuasive writing methods.

Because we use pending Supreme Court cases in my course, I spend a fair amount of time going over my honor code expectations. If you are teaching second or third-year students, you may want to distinguish between typical standards in practice versus standards in academia. On the rare occasions when I have dealt with honor code violations, I always find myself wondering if I could have said anything that might have made a difference. Now, on the first day of class, when I talk about honor code requirements, I go through a small cost-benefit analysis, knowing that someone may be making a decision late at night, without the best decision-making process. I talk in non-identifying ways about the trauma of these violations, and about how the honor code is the law school version of the code of professional responsibility that they must uphold as lawyers. I mention examples of lawyers who have been indicted for spending clients' money. I tell them that just as they may think they are the only ones who will know if they cheat on a paper, soon they will be the only ones who know that they are holding a client's money in trust. In the case of cheating (i.e., looking at professional briefs when they have been forbidden to do so), I remind them that they will know, and that their computers will know. There is usually an impressive moment of silence at this point.

I say, in stark terms, that an incomplete is better than getting caught cheating, a "C" is better than getting caught cheating, even having an "F" on their report card is better than getting caught cheating. I believe that much cheating results from a combination of procrastination, ego, and panic. That is, the student puts off the writing until the only product possible is a bad one, a document that will embarrass the writer. Then he or she panics and tries to avoid the problem by cheating. I talk to the students about the fact that they will _not_ reduce stress by cheating. On the contrary, they will increase their stress, for they will worry even if they are not caught. If they _are_ caught, the stress will be enormous. This discussion may not prevent everyone from cheating, but if someone does get caught and is prosecuted, I at least feel that they have done so with full knowledge of the possible consequences.

Ideas for Audio-Visual Aids or Demonstrations:

Students need to realize that their work will be read by real people, and I find that showing photographs of presumed readers can make a significant difference in their perceptions. I currently show five photographs; you will find them on the book's Companion Website. If you do not have access to a laptop in your classroom, you may wish to print the photographs out (preferably on a color printer) and show them on a document camera. If you have only an overhead projector, you can turn color copies into color transparencies (if you have a color copier).

The first photograph shows an ideal reader: a judge, in robes, with a clean desk, reading with pen in hand to enable note-taking. I talk with the students about whether this represents a realistic view of how judges read briefs.

The second photograph shows a judge with a crowded desk, reading from a stack of briefs. I take a moment to refer to the materials in the text about the reading load of various judges. There is some child's art on the "judge's" bulletin board, and it presents an opportunity to talk about the fact that judges have real lives.

Before showing **the third photograph**, I remind students that the judge may not be the first person to read the brief, and I show a reader, presumably a clerk, struggling with the text. This clerk is a good reader, I point out, and I ask the class why. The correct answer: because the clerk is struggling to understand the text. At this point I engage them in the following discussion, with more or less class participation (or none) depending on the size of the class:

> Presuming that you are not studying for an exam or preparing to be called on, what do you do when you read something that you don't understand? Do you stop to look up certain words? Do you re-read it and try to diagram the sentence? If so, how many times to do you re-read? Or do you just shake your head, and say to yourself, 'Gee, I sure wish I understood this stuff,' as you turn the page? Of course, even this scenario presumes that you _noticed_ that you didn't understand something. How many times do you fail to understand without realizing that you failed to understand?

Chapter One

The fourth photograph shows a law clerk who is less engaged in the text (she is eating while she reads), and I often tell the class the story of a friend of mine who worked as a law clerk in the Sixth Circuit. She was an incredibly diligent worker, but she read the briefs only once, and sometimes less than once (i.e., she stopped before she was through) before deciding whether or not they were going to help her understanding of the case. If the briefs did not appear to be helpful, she saved herself the trouble of trying to decipher them, and did the research and analysis herself. Again, my goal is to impress on the students that their brief must be written so that it will help its intended audience: the judges whose job it is to decide the case, and the clerks who will help them to understand the relevant law and facts.

The fifth photograph shows a (presumed) judge in his "robes" (a bathrobe), asleep in bed, with a brief on his lap. Just before I click on this, I say, "Of course, from what I understand, I think a lot of judges read in their robes" – cut to this photograph of sleeping judge in bathrobe. I point out that with all of these photographs, my goal is not to denigrate the hard work of the judges and clerks, but to show that judges and clerks must make realistic decisions about how to spend the limited time that they have to read the briefs. Again, if it is appropriate, I talk to them about how often they, as law students, take work home that doesn't get done, or try to work and find themselves interrupted by the telephone, the doorbell, or by fatigue. And, FYI, this picture is of my father — I did not go into a real judge's bedroom to take the photograph!

The powerpoint now also contains pictures of "readers" as compared to users. The sixth photograph shows a man in shorts, lying on a couch reading a book. The seventh shows a man in professional dress, lying on the same couch, reading a brief. I use it to contrast the way we read a book and read a brief. The eighth picture shows a clerk sitting at a desk, *using* a brief – that is, searching it for information that he can use to put in the opinion. Again, my goal is to get students to understand that the way *they* read and use opinions is pretty close to the way that judges and clerks read and use briefs.

You may think of other ways to demonstrate the demands on the reader. For example, check out the oral argument docket of the nearest Appellate Court, and the page limits for its briefs. Figure out the total number of pages that one or two weeks of arguments represents, and make a stack that shows that page total. You may have to bring it into the room on a cart. Remind the students that this represents *only* the briefs, and not any record materials, authority cases, or statutes.

At the end of this discussion, students have a reasonable understanding of *why* it is important to write clearly and effectively: because their briefs will be read by real people, busy people who need the briefs to provide a complete and accurate picture of their client's case and the arguments that support it. This leads naturally to a discussion of *how* to use writing process methods to provide an effective brief. If your students have just finished a semester in which they have used writing process principles, you may not need to discuss this at all. If they have a variety of backgrounds in legal writing (i.e., they had one of several different professors who may have used different teaching techniques), you may want to discuss the basics of how the writing process works, perhaps using section 1.3 as a starting point.

It's unrealistic to think that their writing can be understood by a *sleeping* judge, but they should be able to write in a way that any legal reader can understand, and understand easily. So this semester we will work on writing process – first, on gaining an understanding of the legal issues that the case presents, then on how to organize it and present it, and finally, on how to write paragraphs and sentences in the most understandable way.

If your students are unfamiliar with practice documents, you may wish to refer them to Appendix C, which contains the sample briefs. Even students who have experience with office memos and motion briefs are often intimidated by the concept of an appellate brief, and want to know "what one looks like." My assurances that they are rectangular are often ignored, and I find that having a sample to look at calms many of their fears. You will note that the sample briefs are annotated to highlight the strengths and some weaknesses of each of the four samples. If you are teaching this chapter in conjunction with Chapter Two, this introduction can lead naturally into a discussion of some of the peculiarities of appellate practice or motion practice, in particular the concept of standard of review.

Ideas for in-class exercises:

I usually do not conduct any in-class exercises in relation to this chapter. If you wish to do so, you may think about holding a quick group research session on professional responsibility issues, OR you may wish to go to a website that shows the workload of an appellate court, for example: [http://www.uscourts.gov/Home.aspx] frequently offers access to relevant statistics about the workload of the federal courts. Of course, whenever you are thinking of conducting on-line research in class, it is best to do a test run to see what you will find with various searches.

Significant Vocabulary for Chapter One:

Writing process
Macro draft
Micro draft
Reader
User
Cognitivist School of Writing Theory
Social Perspective School of Writing Theory

Chapter Two
Appellate Jurisdiction and Standards of Review

Possible Teaser(s) for Syllabus:

We will discuss the significance of dead fish.
[*See* Section 2.3.1.a]

Learning Goals of Class Meeting:

Help the students understand the concept of Standard of Review and how the most common standards operate, whether in appellate briefs, motion briefs, or both.

Help the students to understand the differences between and among the concepts of appellate standards of review, motion standards of review, and government action standards of review.

Give students a method for determining the appropriate standard of review in their case.

Changes from the Second Edition:

In Chapter 2, relevant citations have been updated. In particular, the discussion of the standard of review for a motion to dismiss has been expanded. In particular, the recent cases from the United States Supreme Court (Twombly and Iqbal) are cited. Also, the text notes that some courts use the terms "pleading standard" and "legal standard" instead of the phrase "standard of review." The discussion of summary judgment motions is also slightly expanded.

Website aids:

N/A

Ideas for Lecture and/or Discussion:

I find that standard of review is one of the harder concepts for students to understand, because it is often not addressed in their other courses, despite the fact that they spend the bulk of their time reading appellate cases. In appellate cases, the Standard of Review is like the poem about the girl with the curl in the middle of her forehead ("forrid"): "When she was good, she was very, very good, and when she was bad, she was horrid." If the standard of review is *de novo*, then it will have almost no impact on the appellate case and need not be dealt with at all after it is announced. If the standard is abuse of discretion or clearly erroneous, however, it will be very significant and may be a big part of the argument. In motion briefs, the standard is the framework for the whole case, but it may or may not be a constant focus of discussion in the argument.

I usually start the discussion by asking about the significance of dead fish (See Section 2.3.1.a). This leads to a discussion of the most common standards, and how standards of review function. Students need to understand that sometimes different standards may apply in the same case, if more than one of the court's decisions affects the appeal. To test their knowledge of the different uses of the term "standard of review," I'll ask how "strict scrutiny" fits in to this mix. If the class seems confused, I may reproduce the chart from the text on the chalkboard or an overhead and go over the differences among the three uses of the term. As noted in the text, this concept can be particularly confusing if a case happens to involve two or more uses of the term.

Whether or not the students have received their case packets, I ask them how they would go about searching for standard of review. If their case is not in federal court, they must first acquaint themselves with the correct labels for the standards of review in their own jurisdiction. (A state practice manual is a good place to start.) Whether they are in federal or state court, if the standard is not evident, they may need to conduct some research. You might engage the class in discussion about how they would accomplish this task. Where would they go? To a federal practice manual? How could they search on-line? You might come up with a couple of different paths for them to follow. For example, if the case involves a review of a decision about standing, they might search for the word "standing" in the same sentence as the phrase "de novo" or "clearly erroneous" or "abuse of discretion." In the alternative, they might consult a practice manual, and search "standing" directly. If the case is a motion case, they could use the title of the motion (e.g., "motion for summary judgment") as a search term, and look for "standard of review" within the sentence or the paragraph. **Caution:** Some students who are writing motion briefs may confuse the appellate standard with the motion standard because they may read appellate decisions that say, e.g., "The standard of review for reviewing a grant of summary judgment is de novo." Be sure that they can distinguish between the standard that the trial court uses when *deciding* the motion, and the standard that the appellate court uses when *reviewing the way in which the trial court decided* the motion.

Ideas for Exercises or Group Work:

I usually do not do exercises at this stage, but a couple of ideas readily suggest themselves. If the students are already working on their own case, you may ask them (either as a class or in groups) to list the decisions of the court below that could affect the outcome of the appeal (e.g., decisions on evidentiary matters, decisions about whether to grant or deny certain motions, decisions about how the law applies to certain facts, or decisions about what did or didn't happen below). Ask them to identify whether each decision is a finding of fact, a conclusion of law, or something else. If you break the students up into groups for this exercise, it may be interesting to see if the groups agree on the decisions made and on how to characterize the decisions.

If the students have not yet received a case to work on, you could **assign readings in Appendix C in advance.** The sample brief "standard of review" sections tend to be vague, and you can use class time to encourage the students to be more specific when they address standard of review in their own briefs. Of course, in order to address it they must understand how the pieces fit together.

For example, you could have them read the Statement of the Case in the <u>Miller v. Albright</u> sample and identify the decisions made by the court below, and possible standard of review issues that the case presents. For example, the statement of the case notes that the defendant appealed the motion to dismiss on three grounds:

> Her appeal presented three separate claims. First, she argued that the district court erred in finding that she lacked standing; second, she argued that 8 U.S.C. § 1409(a)(4) violates the Fifth Amendment's equal protection guarantees; and third, she argued that she meets the requirements of 8 U.S.C. § 1409(a)(4) because the voluntary paternity decree "legitimated" her as of her date of birth.

The primary decision that is being appealed, of course, is the decision on the motion to dismiss, but that decision may be affected by the decisions that supported the decision to grant the motion. The decision as to whether 1409(a)(4) violates equal protection seems to be obviously a conclusion of law. The other decisions may not be as obvious. Is a decision about standing subject to de novo review or abuse of discretion? What would be the policy reasons behind either standard? The decision as to whether the voluntary paternity decree "legitimated" her may seem to some to be a finding of fact, but the issue is not whether she was actually "legitimate," or whether her father was voluntarily assuming paternity. There is no dispute about when and how the paternity decree came into being (those would be factual questions). Instead, the question is how the law applies to that decree, which is obviously a legal question.

Some students find the standard is harder to incorporate into a motion brief than in an appellate brief. An important point to make is that they must be able to connect the argument to the standard in some way. For starters, the students themselves must understand how the pieces fit together. The chapter gives some examples of how writers can incorporate the standard into the argument section.

Ideas for Audio-Visual Aids or Demonstration:

One caveat about spending too much time on standard of review: students may devote too much of their research time to the issue, even if it is not significant in their particular case. Perhaps a good use of class time would be to spend time as a group (or in small groups) planning an on-line research strategy for their particular case, and then chasing down the various dead ends together, arriving at the answer that the students can then include in their briefs.

For example, if you wanted to research the appropriate standard of review for the issue of "standing," you might not find much in the United States Supreme Court on the issue. In addition or in the alternative, you might search a law review database or a federal court of appeals database (because the sheer number of court of appeals decisions might make it more likely that your narrow question had been addressed).

When I research in on-line resources, I try to imagine a sentence that would appear in a case that would give me the answer, e.g., "The issue of standing is reviewed de novo." Or "We review questions of standing using the abuse of discretion standard." I then construct a search using appropriate connectors and synonyms to find the appropriate cases. Of course, whenever you are thinking of conducting on-line research in class, it is best to do a test run to see what you will find with various searches.

Significant Vocabulary for Chapter Two:

Appellate Standard of Review
Clearly Erroneous
De Novo
Plenary Review
Abuse of Discretion
Motion Standard of Review
Pleading Standard
Legal Standard

Chapter Three
Before You Write

Possible Teaser(s) for Syllabus:

Please be able to explain why research is like dating and writing is like marriage
[*See* Section 3.4]
Identify courts from which you might harvest arguments.
[*See* Section 3.3.3]

Learning Goals:

Importance of preparation before research
Identifying questions that need researching
Thinking abstractly about the problem as a way of helping to identify relevant authorities while
      researching
Identifying optimal and practical research results, including extra-legal sources
Understanding the significance of mandatory v. nonmandatory authorities
Understanding how to *develop* an argument that another court has referenced (aka "harvesting"
arguments)

Changes from Second Edition:

The term "super search terms" has been changed to "foundational search terms." The text
includes an expanded discussion of how to harvest arguments, and both good and bad examples of
harvesting an argument. The chapter also includes a reference to some of the difficulties students
may have when transferring from Google to other search methods.

Powerpoint:

The book's website will contain a powerpoint that illustrates how to "harvest" an
argument. It uses the same example that is contained in the text, but it goes into a bit more
detail. You may wish to use this example, or create your own based on this one. The
powerpoint also tries to drive home the idea of the power of authority by showing the same quote
on two slides and asking students to identify what the difference is. The correct answer is that
the identical quotes come from briefs directed at two different courts. It is meant to teach
students that a statement that is authoritative in one court can be merely mildly persuasive in
another. The powerpoint also gives illustrations of faux secondary authorities of varying levels
of validity.

Ideas for Lecture and/or Discussion:

At this stage, students should have a good idea about methods for conducting legal
research. If they have never researched a case to present to a court of last resort, however, they
may still be thinking inside the box and looking for the mandatory, on-point case. My goal in
this class is not to talk overmuch about different methods of conducting legal research, but to

talk about having an effective point of view before researching. To this end, I try to get students to talk in detail about the case itself, trying to identify the broad themes and ideas that the facts and decisions below present.

The chapter talks about the <u>Coors</u> case and how students could move from a case about commercial speech to thinking about "vices that the government regulates." If the students have a fourth amendment case involving a search of an automobile that revealed drugs, for example, there might be several ideas to track down. Authorities dealing with the "war on drugs," authorities dealing with automobile searches, authorities dealing with the limits of the fourth amendment, authorities dealing with abuse of police power, etc. I spend a lot of time in this class asking "what is this case about?" To stimulate discussion, I might ask, "what do the petitioners think this case is about?" "What do the respondents think this case is about?" (I ask this question even if I have not yet assigned students to a particular side of the case.)

Possible pre-class assignments in addition to the readings:

The week before this class meets, I make the following assignment (and post it on the course website):

Please bring a printed/written copy of the following to class:

1. Identify at least 3 facts that might be significant to your side's argument.
2. Identify the two most significant authorities you are aware of to date (these may be from the lower court decision or may be things you have found on your own). Be able to explain why they are significant.
3. Identify at least 3 specific avenues for research (e.g., shepardize/keycite X case from lower court decision, look for law review article about Z, look for Supreme Court cases in Q area). Be able to explain your choices.
4. Identify at least 3 legal/factual/policy categories that you might fit the case into.
E.g., the issue in the Chickasaw Nation case was how to interpret a tax law that applied to Indian tribes. 3 categories might be: tax law, laws/policies dealing with native American issues, and statutory construction issues.

If you do not have these items in writing, you will be turned away from the class with an unexcused absence.

[As noted above in the section on group work, there are alternatives to the "turn away" method. For example, you could have the students e-mail you the lists the day before class; in the alternative, you could use class time to have the students do individual brainstorming to create the lists above before the group work.]

Audio-visual aids or demonstrations:

I find that the chalkboard is best for leading a discussion of this type; others might be more at home with other media.

Possible group exercises/Discussion:

1. Brainstorming on research ideas and themes:

In addition to discussions based on the list above, the teacher could divide the class into groups of petitioners and respondents, and ask each group to share their prepared lists and then rank the items on them. In addition or in the alternative, you might ask them to come up with possible "extra-legal" research or ideas. Remind the students that the list should help them both with their research and with the themes of their argument.

For example, if students on either side of <u>Miller v. Albright</u> were asked to come up with a list of categories that the case could fit in and relevant extra-legal sources, the lists might look like this:

<u>Miller</u>
Equal protection
"Illegitimacy"
sex discrimination
discrimination based on nationality?
discrimination against fathers
fathers' rights
Age discrimination?
sex stereotypes
limits on Congressional authority
      Extra legal sources:
           studies on benefits of fathers developing relationships with children later in life
           studies on accuracy of DNA testing to identify fathers

<u>Albright</u>
Equal protection
immigration law
Congressional authority over immigration
validity of long-standing precedent
bona fide differences between the sexes
regulation of military families?
illegitimacy
sex discrimination
      Extra-legal sources
           numbers of immigrants who claim a connection that later proves to be false.
           Expense of DNA testing?
           numbers of children born to Serviceman fathers?

Note that there is some overlap on these lists; students should realize that they may have to research aspects of the case that aren't the "best" from their client's point of view. From the lists above, students conducting legal research in <u>Miller v. Albright</u> would be encouraged to look beyond on-point cases to cases that address the themes that are important to their client's argument.

After the students complete the lists, take time to share with the whole class, perhaps by putting petitioner lists on one side of the board and respondent lists on the other. The first group finished for each party could write their entire list on the board, while later groups could check the items that their group also identified, and add items not already on the list. In the alternative, you could put the lists on the board, calling on students from the different groups as you compile the different lists. In this way, students would see how much agreement there is in the class on the themes and issues that the case presents. Sophie Sparrow recommends carefully controlling the time spent in groups. For example, rather than having the groups spend twenty minutes working on four lists, and then spending ten minutes sharing, tell the students, e.g., "Okay, spend four minutes talking about the 3 most important facts in the case, in rank order. Go!" Exactly four minutes later, spend three minutes sharing. That would give you time to have discussion and sharing of 4 lists. (Of course, over-preparing is allowed; you may decide to use this method with only a couple of the prepared lists.)

After you have discussed the themes and ideas, take some time to discuss methods of researching. Do the students know enough about this area of law to go directly to primary authorities? Should they do some background reading first? Look at the list of possible extra-legal sources. How would they support the principle or policy behind the client's argument? If you believe that extra-legal resources or policy arguments would be particularly important, you might want to recommend that your students read one of the following articles by Ellie Margolis, which are particularly relevant to policy arguments:

Ellie Margolis, *Closing the Floodgates: Making Persuasive Policy Arguments in Appellate Briefs*, 62 Mont. L. Rev. 60 (2001).

Ellie Margolis, *Beyond Brandeis: Exploring the Uses of Non-Legal Materials in Appellate Briefs*, 34 U.S. F. L. Rev. 197 (2000).

2. <u>Discussion of how to take notes on cases:</u>

Ideally, students will have learned organized ways for taking notes on cases in the previous semester. If there is any doubt, however, or if you wish to reinforce these lessons, you might want to spend some time on reading and note-taking as part of legal research. Many legal writing faculty have developed research charts that students can use to take notes on the cases they find in their research. A possibility appears below, but you may have found or developed another that better meets your expectations. As with any chart of this type, you should stress precision in completing the chart (e.g., that they should note the court because it determines the weight of the authority, that they should include pinpoint citations for any information). It is set up in a dozen rows with two columns for ease of reproduction, but the better format would be a dozen columns with two rows, for ease of cross-reference (and an excel spreadsheet may well be better than a word-processing file).

Chapter Three

If there is a case that you think everyone should read, you might want to spend class time having the students complete the chart below for that case. The chart presumes that some overlap is possible, or even desirable, and that students might want to make connections between the columns explicit. For example, Items 5, 6, 7, and 8 should be related to each other. Item 5 asks the student to identify issues, themes, or policies that the case is useful for. Once that happens, the student should identify relevant phrases-that-pay for those items (Item 6), what decisions the court made on each of those issues (Item 7), and whether there are any quotable rules or other language relevant to those issues (Item 8). Of course, the items need not be completed in numerical order. In some cases, the student might first identify a quotable rule or other language (Item 8); the student could then ask "what issue is that quote relevant to?" and work from there to complete Items 5, 6, and 7. In the same way, the student might first identify a phrase-that-pays (Item 6) or a particular holding or finding (Item 7), and work from that starting point to fill in the rest of the items. Items 9 and 10 are relatively clear (they ask students to identify factual and issue-based analogies and distinctions), but you may wish to have some discussion about Item 11, which asks whether it would be "okay" (i.e., good for the client) if the rule from the case were to be applied to the client's case.

For example, some students presume that if their client is a nun, they don't want to cite any cases in which the nun loses. They need to be encouraged to recognize that sometimes the nun lost because she had a bad case, whereas their nun might have a good case. E.g., if the nun in the authority case was beating the aardvark with a stick and the aardvark bit her, that case does not hurt their client if their client is a nun who was walking on a public sidewalk and was attacked by an aardvark whose owner let it wander free.

As noted above, the handout example shows a word-processing file where an excel spreadsheet may well be preferable. The rows can be turned into columns, and the students could line up the relevant information – i.e., the relevant issue next to its phrase-that-pays next to the decision the court made on it next to the quotable language, etc.

Significant vocabulary for Chapter Three:
Abstract of the Record
Abstraction Ladder
"Foundational Search Terms"
Harvesting arguments
Theme
Policy arguments

1. Case name and full citation in correct format:	
2. Court & Date:	
3. Fact Summary:	
4. Disposition of Case:	
5. Issues/Themes/ Policies this case is useful for:	
6. Phrases-that-pay:	
7. Relevant Findings/ Holdings/Dicta:	
8. Quotable rules, reasoning, or other language:	
9. How facts are analogous/ distinguishable	
10. How issues are analogous/ distinguishable	
11. Okay if rule(s) from this case applies here?	
12. Update completed? (I.e., Keycite, Shepards)	
13. Other information needed:	

Chapter Four
Facing the Blank Page

Possible Teaser for Syllabus:

> We will discuss how using the phrase-that-pays pays off.
> [*See* Section 4.1.1]
> We will discuss how private memos can help prevent writer's block
> [*See* Section 4.2]

Learning Goals:

Helping students to move from research to writing
Helping students to identify structure before, during, and after the first draft
Identifying the phrase-that-pays
Avoiding writer's block

Changes from the Second Edition:

Chapter 4 includes no significant changes.

Audio-visual aids:

If you spend class time discussing the method of brainstorming and planning mentioned in the book, you might want to create an overhead that shows the "list of points the court must agree with," the "reverse roadmap," and/or the "working outline." Of course, you could have students create one or more of these documents focused on their case, either alone, as an in-class exercise, or both.

Possible pre-class assignments in addition to the readings:

You could ask the class to make a list of rules, policies, and other assertions that could govern this case. They could either bring the list to class or e-mail it to you in advance of class. If you plan to have them do some or all of this work in class (or to revisit the work in a small-group setting), you might ask them to bring their significant authorities to the class.

Ideas for Lecture and Discussion:

Many students are very intimidated by the thought of moving from research to writing. The pile of printed-out cases grows and grows in the corner of their carrel or their bedroom, until the thought of starting to write becomes overwhelming. This may be the biggest research project that students have ever tackled, and so the logistics of organizing the information may be hard to get a handle on. You may wish to lead a discussion about how people have organized big projects in the past. This could lead naturally to one of the suggested exercises below.

At some point in the class, you may wish to discuss your expectations, if any, as to the "private memos" discussed in the book. I find them to be very helpful reading when I review the papers, because they often reveal the root of the student's problem. If you want a more formal document, you may not want students to include private memos, and so you should tell them so. On the other hand, you may want to *require* at least one private memo, or private memos that answer certain specific questions, e.g., "identify the page on which your best-written argument begins. Why is it your best argument?" OR "Which part of the argument was hardest for you to write? What was difficult about it?" It may be helpful to reassure students that you don't require the private memos to be anything formal, and you may want to create or quote from fictional private memos to make this point: "The hardest part for me was the policy argument I tried to make about the fourth amendment. It seemed that all of the authorities were the same as my other sections, and I felt like I was repeating myself. Should I take out the policy argument, or just blend it into the other sections?"

In-class exercises or group work:

Becky Cochran, of the University of Dayton, recommends having the students work together to move from research to outlining. If the students should have their research done by this point, you may wish to **require them to bring in their stacks of cases.** Then you can put them in petitioner and respondent groups and have them come up with a tentative outline of points that they plan to discuss. An advantage to having them do this as an in-class exercise is that some of them may do it with pen and ink as opposed to the computer screen. Using hands and paper instead of fingers and keyboards can help students to see their case differently both literally and figuratively. You may wish to circulate around the room and help them as they work out the points and, more importantly, the relationships between and among those points. In the alternative

If it is not practical to have students work on their own case, you might try this simple exercise. It requires **preparing a handout or an overhead.** Although a handout makes the first part of the exercise easier, you may want to collect the handout before the second part of the exercise. The statute's text is repeated below for easy copying.

1. Have them read the statute below. It governs liability of a dog owner or keeper for injuries to someone who is bitten by a dog.

2. After the students have read the statute, ask them to tell you various things that might need to be proved to establish liability or lack of liability. I give them *no facts* at this point. I write these things scattered all over the board, taking care to *separate* related items. (I try to leave half the board clean for me to use later.)

3. Once they have given me the entire list, I ask them to turn the statute over. I then tell them that these scattered ideas could be much like the results of their research in this area *if the statute did not exist.* I sometimes write pretend case names under several of the elements, taking care to repeat case names in a realistic fashion – i.e., it would be logical for the same case to address multiple sub-parts of a rule.

4. Then I point out that in many situations, the parties won't need to prove the whole list

because some of the items will be irrelevant. So I ask them to identify the *categories* of things that need to be proven – how many different things need to be established? How do the categories and the elements from the categories fit together? At this point, you could have students work in groups, or you could just lead the class in discussion. A common answer is 3 (of course, some people might break it down differently, but I think 3 is pretty reasonable): 1) something about an owner-type relationship between the person and the dog, 2) something about the dog causing harm, and 3) something about that the injury was NOT the fault of the person who was bitten. So at this point they have a three-part outline with numerous sub-parts. And if I am writing the outline on the board, I move all of the sub-parts over to the appropriate category. I take care to keep the case names with each sup-part, so I can reinforce the concept of organizing around issues and not around cases.

5. I then give them a hypothetical set of facts (also below) and have them decide which sub-parts can be eliminated because they're irrelevant to the client's case. The facts are not that important; I sometimes give them the facts orally.

The Statute:
Ohio Revised Code § 955.28(B) provides:

The owner, keeper, or harborer of a dog is liable in damages for any injury, death, or loss to person or property that is caused by the dog, unless the injury, death or loss was caused to the person or property of an individual who, at the time, was committing or attempting to commit a trespass or other criminal offense on the property of the owner, keeper, or harborer, or was committing or attempting to commit a criminal offense against any person, or was teasing, tormenting, or abusing the dog on the owner's, keeper's, or harborer's property.

Here's an example of an organized list (of course, you would un-organize it on the board):

You are liable if

A) You have ONE of the following relationships to a dog:
1. You are the owner of the dog, or
2. You are the keeper of the dog, or
3. You are the harborer of the dog
AND

B) ONE of the following is true:
1. the dog caused injury to a person
2. the dog caused death to a person
3. the dog caused loss to a person
4. the dog caused loss to property
AND

C) The individual who suffered the harm described in B was NOT, at the time of the harm, doing even ONE of the following:
1. Committing a trespass on the property of the person in A or

2. Attempting to commit a trespass on the property of the person in A or
3. Committing another criminal offense on the property of the person in A or
4. Attempting to commit another criminal offense on the property of the person in A or
5. Committing a criminal offense against any person or
6. Attempting to commit a criminal offense against any person, or
7. teasing the dog on the property of the person in A or
8. tormenting the dog on the property of the person in A or
9. abusing the dog on the property of the person in A.

Possible facts: Daniel Yeary is coming from out of town to attend a family funeral. He plans to go to his brother's house (Armand Yeary), but gets confused in the subdivision and turns down "Spring Grove Lane" instead of "Spring Brook Lane." Goes to the home of David Pillion, who has a dog named Thurber. Pillion's house is open because he expects his son late that night. Daniel Yeary enters what he thinks is his brother's house and is attacked by Thurber, who bites Yeary's leg, requiring ten stitches. Is Pillion liable?

Now their outline shrinks. They'd have to prove three things:

A) Pillion is owner (easy)
B) dog caused injury to person (easy)
C) Yeary was committing a trespass or other criminal offense (this one is a little harder: does the statute include only criminal trespass -- which this probably wasn't -- or criminal and civil?)

You can also use the exercise to discuss using phrases-that-pay to organize your analysis. E.g., if "harm" were at issue (does a scratch on the arm constitute "harm") *and* "causation" were at issue, section B would have to broken into two sub-parts. You can also use the exercise to discuss what you have to *say* in a brief vs. what you have to *prove*. A brief-writer could probably take care of A & B in introductory material, doing a full CREXAC only on C.

Significant Vocabulary for Chapter Four:

Phrase-that-pays
Brainstorming
Reverse Roadmap
Private memos

Other materials for handouts or overheads:

1. List of Points that a court must agree with (from text)
2. "Reverse Roadmap" (from text)
3. Working outline (from text)
****

List of points that court must agree with:

1. Court should reverse decision below.

2. Statute is unconstitutional.

3. Statute discriminates on the basis of gender

4. Court should scrutinize the statute under intermediate level of scrutiny

5. Statute fails the intermediate scrutiny test

6. Statute is even unconstitutional under rational basis-type scrutiny

7. Court should not defer to Congress even though this is an immigration law

8. The statute is not substantially related to the achievement of the government's objective

9. There is not an "exceedingly persuasive justification" for the distinction between the children of the two types of parents.

10. It is not rational to distinguish between children of U.S. citizen fathers and children of U.S. citizen mothers.

11. Stopping gender discrimination and "illegitimacy" discrimination is more important than allowing Congress control over immigration.

12. Someone who is a child of a U.S. citizen is not an "immigrant" and so a statute that regulates such a person is not an immigration statute.

13. Biological parent-child relationships are important.

This court should reverse the decision below. In order to decide to reverse, they have to agree that 1409 is unconstitutional.

In order to agree that 1409 is unconstitutional they either have to agree that it violates the intermediate scrutiny test or that it violates the rational basis test.

In order to agree that it violates the intermediate scrutiny test they first have to agree that the intermediate scrutiny test applies. In order to agree that the intermediate scrutiny test applies, they have to agree that the statute discriminates on the basis of gender.

They would also have to agree that this is not an immigration statute, so they don't have to defer to Congress and therefore apply an easier test, OR they have to agree that even if it is an immigration statute, the fact that it discriminates on the basis of gender is more significant.

Now, in order to agree that the statute *fails* the intermediate scrutiny test, they have to agree both that there's no substantial relationship between the discrimination in the statute and the achievement of the government's goals *and* that there's no exceedingly persuasive justification for the statute.

In order to agree that it violates the rational basis test, they first have to agree that this is the correct test to apply, which means that they think that immigration law is more important than gender law. In order to agree that it violates the rational basis test, they first have to agree that Congress had no rational reason for the law.

It might help them agree that 1409 is unconstitutional if they agree that biological parent-child relationships are important, or reuniting parents and children is important.

Working Outline

I. This court should reverse because 1409 is unconstitutional

    A. This court should apply an intermediate scrutiny test.

        1. The statute discriminates on the basis of gender
        2. This is not an immigration statute, so no special deference to Congress is needed.
        3. Even if it is an immigration statute, fighting gender discrimination and illegitimacy discrimination trumps immigration.

    B. This statute fails the intermediate scrutiny test

        1. There's no substantial relationship between the discrimination in the statute and the achievement of the government's goals.
        2. There's no exceedingly persuasive justification for the statute.

    C. Even if this court applies the rational basis-type test, the statute still fails because there's no rational relationship between encouraging ties between parents and children and requiring a father to establish ties in a different way than mothers do.

Chapter Five
Drafting the Argument

Possible Teaser(s) for Syllabus:

Be able to explain why CREXAC will not make your writing boring.
[Section 5.1.1 (box)]
Be able to explain when a law is a fact.
[5.1.4(c)]

Teaching Goals:

Helping Students to Understand the CREXAC formula, particularly
    Various ways that the rule may need to be stated
    How to explain the rule
    How to apply the rule to the facts
        How to use facts with questions of law
        How to use "facts" with statutory interpretation issues

Noting the difference between the unique formula for their case (which, ideally, they crafted from the "working outline" chapter) and the re-usable CREXAC formula, that can be used in any unit of discourse.

Helping students to understand when a CREXAC unit of discourse is or is not needed

Helping students to understand the importance of dealing with opponent's arguments

Changes from Second Edition:

      Chapter 5 includes two significant changes. First, it includes a discussion of when *not* to use the CREXAC formula, and introduces four labels to use to describe the ways in which a writer can report the result of the analysis of a legal issue: (1) Ignore, (2) Tell (one-sentence statement), (3) Clarify (CRAC analysis), and (4) Prove (CREXAC analysis). Further, Chapter 5 now includes a section on dealing with the opponent's arguments. This section is an expanded discussion of the section on dealing with an opponent's *authorities* that was included in chapter 6 in previous editions. This section discusses Professor Kathryn Stanchi's scholarship on this issue. It also notes that the locus of the controversy may dictate where it is discussed. For example, if the parties disagree on what the rule is, the writer will address the opponent's argument differently than if they disagree on how the rule applies.

Possible pre-class homework in addition to the readings:

      Particularly if you worked with students on creating an outline the previous week, ask students to pick one heading and write up a CREXAC unit of discourse. They can e-mail it to you the day before class, and you can go through them to find good and classic bad examples to work with. *See* introductory material above, for ideas on using student work as an exemplar in class.

Audio-Visual Aids:

On the Book's website, you will find a powerpoint about how to create a first draft. As with all powerpoints, you can use it to display the points, or you can ask students for the points and then display them.

Ideas for Lecture/Discussion & Demonstration:

If your students are familiar with analytical formulas, your discussion may be fairly simple, although you will want to note any changes in vocabulary. For example, what this book (and others) refer to as "explanation" is what others call "rule proof" or the "analogous cases section." The term "phrase that pays," which others call "key terms," will probably be new. To make sure everyone is one the same page, I sometimes begin with a quick discussion of the "Socrates" illustration of the formula, pointing out that the explanation section is what separates a pure syllogism from legal analysis: the explanation is the bridge between the rule and the application. I sometimes display (or even hand out) a quasi-mathematical version of the formula, which can help some students to understand how it works.

Conclusion:
    This Court should find Result.
        [or, This Court should find not-Result.]

Rule:
    If Phrase-that-pays exists, then result occurs.

Explanation:
    In <u>Authoritycase.1</u>, court held that phrase-that-pays existed because facts + reasoning.
        [more authorities about the phrase-that-pays existing, if needed]

    In <u>Authoritycase.B</u>, court held that phrase that pays did <u>not</u> exist because facts + reasoning.

        [more authorities about the phrase–that-pays not existing, if needed]

Application:
    Phrase-that-pays = my case facts.
        [or, Phrase-that-pays ≠ my case facts]
        [details about facts as needed]

        If needed:
            Unlike [party or thing] in <u>Authoritycase.1</u>, [party or thing] in my case did not . . . .

Like [party or thing] in <u>Authoritycase.B</u>, [party or thing] in my case did . . . .

Connection-Conclusion:
Therefore, because phrase-that-pays exists, result should occur.
[or, Therefore, because phrase-that-pays does not exist, result should not occur.]

If appropriate:

Because result should occur, case should be resolved in X's favor.

Because the explanation section is often the hardest thing for students to understand, I spend the most time on that point. First, I try to get them to understand how to identify the phrase-that-pays; second, I discuss how much explanation to provide for the phrase-that-pays, and finally, I illustrate an actual explanation section. The Sarah Student brief in Appendix C (<u>Minnesota v. Carter</u>, petitioner) makes good use of phrases-that-pay and provides a strong explanation in almost every section. You may wish to use section I.C. to illustrate the formula. (An earlier version of section I.C. is reprinted in the manual if you wish to create a handout.)

To work on identifying the phrase-that-pays, you may wish to place a rule up on the overhead in two forms: first, the way it might be written in a brief; second, the same rule written as an if-then statement. For example, the rule from section I.C. of the first brief in Appendix C is written in the brief this way:

An individual seeking to establish that he possessed a legitimate expectation of privacy must first demonstrate that he possessed an "actual (subjective) expectation of privacy."

The same rule as an if-then statement:

If an individual has an "actual (subjective) expectation of privacy," he can demonstrate that he has a legitimate expectation of privacy.

(I use the word "can" here because the actual expectation of privacy is not the only requirement of a legitimate expectation of privacy.)

Next, ask the students what the brief-writer is trying to prove. In this case, she's trying to prove that the respondents did *not* have an actual subjective expectation of privacy, and the phrase-that-pays is "actual, subjective expectation of privacy."

If you wish to further demonstrate finding the phrase-that-pays, you can look to other sections of the Sarah Student brief, or other sample briefs, and find the phrases-that-pay in the rule statements there. In addition or in the alternative, if one of the rules in the students' case is fairly standard – that is, you would predict that most students would be stating the rule in the same way – AND if you are confident that the students have found that rule by this point in their research, you may want to put the students' actual rule up on the overhead projector and ask the students to change it into an if-then clause and then to identify the phrase-that-pays. Although some teachers worry about "giving away" too much with this method, it may be appropriate if the students' case has multiple rules. Explicit discussion of one rule in class will demonstrate the method without doing all of the work for the students – they will still have to handle all of the other rules in their case.

You may also wish to address how to decide how much explanation of the phrase-that-pays to provide. Although the text provides sufficient information, giving a visual image can help some students to understand the concept. Thus, you may wish to place the axes (shown below) on the overhead and note the two questions that will help the writer to decide how much explanation to provide. The higher the phrase-that-pays is on the "controversial" axis, and the farther out the phrase-that-pays is on the "abstract" axis, the more explanation is needed. On the other hand, if the phrase-that-pays is both concrete *and* not controversial (as perhaps the concept of "owner" is in the dog bite fact pattern noted in Chapter Four), very little or no explanation would be needed.

This same continuum can be used to help students decide how much detail to provide in the application section of the document. The more abstract and, particularly, the more controversial the application of the phrase-that-pays is, the more detail the writer will need to provide in the application section, and the more likely it is that the writer will want to analogize or distinguish relevant authority cases.

Of course, this method is *faux* math; the writer is merely guessing at the point on the axis. However, filling in the axes by drawing various lines representing various possibilities (concrete but controversial, abstract but not controversial, etc.) helps some students to recognize that how they use the CREXAC formula will vary according to the demands of each issue.

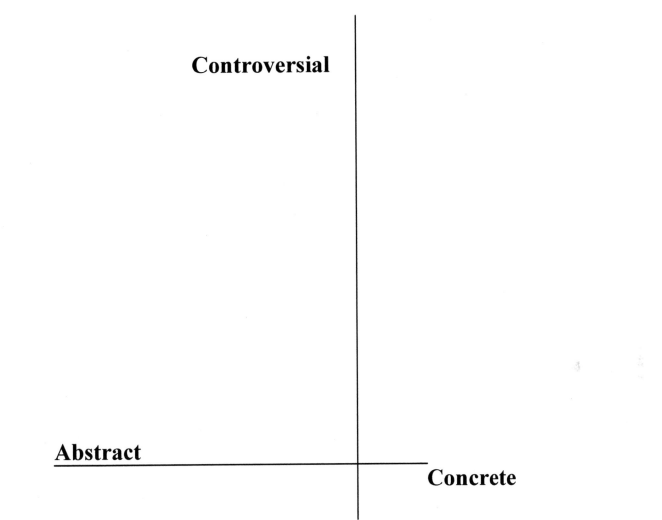

If your students are particularly concerned about their writing being 'boring' if they use the CREXAC formula for each section, you may wish to show the chart below, which illustrates the ways in which the CREXAC formula combines fixed and variable elements:

Fixed:	**Rule**	**Explanation**	**Application**
Variable:	Existing common-law rule	Level of detail	Level of detail
			Type of facts
		Illustrative cases	Use of analogies or
	Induced C/L rule	Definitions	distinctions
	Constitution	Legislative History	
	Policy Rule	Other	
	Statute		
	Regulation		
	Other		

A version of this chart appears in the related powerpoint.

Dealing with negative authority.

The textbook illustrates a somewhat indirect way of dealing with negative issues and authorities. In the alternative, you might want to ask your students to compare the ways in which the Sarah Student (petitioner) and Susan Scholar (respondents) briefs address the Olson decision's relevance in Minnesota v. Carter. Each brief highlights the aspects of the decision that are most positive for its client and directs the Court's attention to its own view of the meaning of the case:

Excerpt from Petitioner's brief:

1. The Olson rule dictates that only overnight guests have a connection to a premises that gives rise to a legitimate expectation of privacy.

Respondents, who introduced no evidence that they were anything other than temporary, transient visitors on the premises for the sole purpose of conducting illegal business, simply do not belong to the class of individuals who have an expectation of privacy that society is prepared to recognize as reasonable. Therefore, they do not have a legitimate expectation of privacy in Thompson's apartment and cannot assert a Fourth Amendment challenge to any alleged search of the premises.

In Minnesota v. Olson, 495 U.S.91, 96-97 (1990), this Court established the rule that "status as an overnight guest is alone enough to show that [the defendant] had an expectation of privacy in the home that society is prepared to recognize as reasonable." In Olson, the Court found that a defendant suspected of driving the getaway car used in a robbery-murder had a legitimate expectation of privacy in his girlfriend's duplex sufficient to challenge a warrantless entry into the duplex.

Id. at ??. Olson, who had been at the duplex for several days, had a change of clothes at the duplex and had spent the previous night there. Id. at 97 n.6. This Court reasoned that, because staying overnight with a host is a socially necessary practice and because all citizens share the expectation that an overnight guest's host will respect the guest's privacy, Olson had a sufficient interest in his girlfriend's home to assert a Fourth Amendment challenge. Id. at 98-99. His expectation of privacy was one that society recognizes as reasonable. Id.

Though some lower courts have been confused as to the scope of the Olson rule, the reasoning in Olson and this Court's emphasis on Olson's overnight status indicate that the holding does not extend to invitees who are not overnight guests.

In establishing the rule that overnight guests have a legitimate expectation of privacy sufficient to challenge a Fourth Amendment search, the Olson Court repeatedly emphasized the overnight nature of the defendant's stay, thus illustrating that the holding does not cover a shorter-term guest. Id. at 97-100. No language in the opinion expressly states that the holding extends beyond overnight guests. The Court's reasoning and examples indicate that the Fourth Amendment protects only those who permanently reside on the premises and those who expect the same protection because they reside on the premises overnight.

The Olson Court discussed at length the social custom of staying overnight with friends or family when traveling to a strange city and the concomitant expectation of privacy that comes with seeking overnight shelter in another's home. The Court reasoned that an expectation of privacy arises because "[we] are at our most vulnerable when we are asleep because we cannot monitor our own safety or the security of our belongings." Id. at 99. While the police found Olson in his host's closet at 3 p.m., the Court's analysis indicated that he had earned the right to assert Fourth Amendment rights in the home because he was an overnight guest in the home the night before. Id.

The factors that gave Olson the right to challenge a search of the residence all hinged on his overnight status. The overnight guest, not the shorter-term invitee, will have a "measure of control over the premises" when "the host is away or asleep." Id. at 99. The overnight guest, not the short-er term invitee, is most likely not to "be confined to a restricted area of the house." Id. The overnight guest, not the shorter-term invitee, has a host who is "willing to share his house and his privacy with his guest." Id.

Furthermore, a significant number of courts that have examined Olson have applied the Olson rule narrowly. Several courts have held that temporary, non-overnight presence for the purpose of illegal drug activity clearly falls outside of the Olson rule. See. e.g., Terry v. Martin, 120 F.3d 661, 664 (7th Cir. 1997) (holding that the legitimate expectation of privacy realized by overnight guests did not extend to confer Fourth Amendment standing on temporary visitors present in an apartment for the purpose of buying heroin); <u>United States v. Hicks</u>, 978 F.2d 722, 724 (D.C. Cir. 1992) (holding that a guest who used an apartment to distribute cocaine had no legitimate expectation of privacy).

Additionally, a number of lower courts have flatly declined to extend <u>Olson</u> to casual or temporary visitors. <u>See</u> <u>State v. Wise</u>, 879 S. W.2d 494, 505 (Mo. 1994) (holding that a defendant who was in an apartment to use the telephone had no legitimate expectation of privacy); <u>Villarreal v. State</u>, 893 S.W.2d 559, 561 (Texas Ct. App. 1994) (declining to extend the <u>Olson</u> expectation to an invited guest who had not stayed overnight but "was welcome to stay if he wanted to"). Some courts have even declined to extend <u>Olson</u> to cover party guests. <u>See</u>, <u>e.g.</u>, <u>Fisher v. State</u>, 665 So.2d 1014 (Ct. App. Ala. 1995); <u>Lewis v. United States</u>, 594 A.2d 542, 546 (D.C. 1991). For example, in <u>Lewis</u>, the court held that a party guest who happened to fall asleep for several hours in a bedroom could not assert a Fourth Amendment challenge to a search of the apartment. <u>Id.</u> at 545. The court ruled that because Lewis offered no evidence that he had been invited to spend the night or intended to do so, he had not shown a legitimate expectation of privacy. <u>Id.</u> The court reasoned that a mere guest who is not spending the night is substantially different from the overnight guest who receives standing under <u>Olson</u>. <u>Id.</u>

In the present case, the record bears no evidence that Respondents were invited overnight guests. <u>See</u> Record E-4. Respondents were not lessees of the apartment. Record G-5. While Respondents were residents of another state, the record provides no evidence as to Respondents' status in the apartment or any link they may have had with it or with the lessee. <u>See</u> Record E-3. Indeed, the only evidence of Respondents' connection to the apartment is the police offer's testimony that he saw Respondents bagging cocaine inside the apartment for a period of 15 minutes. Record E-3. The sparseness of the record and the complete absence of evidence that Respondents intended to spend the night lead only to the conclusion that Respondents were mere temporary visitors who could not claim any parallel characteristics to the overnight guest in <u>Olson</u>. Record E-8.

The Minnesota Supreme Court conceded that "it is undisputed that Carter failed to produce any evidence that he was a 'guest' of Thompson's, let alone an 'overnight guest.'" <u>State v. Carter</u>, 569 N.W.2d 169, 175 (Minn. 1997). Given this Court's emphasis on the special privacy concerns of sleeping guests and the social custom of staying overnight, Respondents do not fall within the <u>Olson</u> rule and cannot claim an expectation of privacy that society is prepared to recognize as reasonable. Thus, they have no legitimate expectation of privacy and are not entitled to claim the protection of an Amendment that was not designed for their use.

Excerpt from Respondents' brief:

A. A person has a legitimate and reasonable expectation of privacy that

society is prepared to acknowledge while he is an invited guest in another person's private residence.

When the Respondents in this case left the public streets and entered the private home of their host, they assumed a legitimate expectation of privacy: that society would give them protection against unwarranted government observation. This Court has said that people like the Respondents will be recognized as having a legitimate expectation of privacy if they demonstrate an expectation that their activities are treated as private, and if it can be shown that society will find that expectation to be reasonable in the given situation. Katz v. United States, 389 U.S. 347, 361 (1967) (Harlan, J., concurring). In Katz, conversations obtained by FBI wiretapping efforts could not be used as evidence to convict a man for transmitting wagering information by public telephone because the defendant clearly demonstrated a legitimate expectation of privacy while using the public telephone. Id. at 348.

This Court reasoned that a person who makes use of a public telephone is surely the type of person who has a legitimate expectation of privacy because most people, when they enter a phone booth and shut the door, assume no one else is listening to the conversation. Id. at 361. Thus, even though a phone booth is accessible to the public, it can also be a temporary private place where the current occupant legitimately expects privacy.

Legitimate expectations of privacy and society's acceptance of those expectations are used by this Court to determine when the protection of the Fourth Amendment goes beyond one's own home, and in which places a person is rightfully protected from unwarranted intrusions by the government. For example, in 1990, this Court held that an overnight guest has a legitimate expectation of privacy in his host's home. Minnesota v. Olson, 495 U.S. 91, 98 (1990). The Olson Court held that Olson's unwarranted arrest was an illegal seizure because Olson, as an invited overnight guest in the apartment, had a sufficient interest in the privacy of his host's home to be free from unwarranted search and seizure. Id. at 96-97. Furthermore, that subjective expectation of privacy was found to be reasonable because society is known to recognize the social custom of staying overnight in another's home. "We will all be hosts and we will all be guests many times in our lives. From either perspective, we think that society recognizes that a houseguest has a legitimate expectation of privacy in his host's home." Id. at 98.

Olson did not specifically require a person to be an overnight guest or even a guest for a legitimate privacy expectation.[21] The legitimacy of Olson's

---

[2] This Court recognized that the status of overnight guest in Olson was enough to show he had a legitimate expectation of privacy. However, the analysis did not rest wholly on whether or not he was an overnight guest, but said an unlawfully searched overnight guest was one example of "a mistaken premise that a place must be one's 'home' in order for one to have a legitimate expectation of privacy there." Id. at 96. Thus, a person can have a legitimate expectation of privacy in places other than his own home, and Olson was one example where the defendant demonstrated such a legitimate expectation. Olson left open the interpretation of what other

expectation was upheld, not specifically because he was a guest, but because the circumstances in which the police intruded upon him are the type in which most people would normally expect to enjoy a feeling of privacy. Id. at 96-97. This was also true in Katz, where a privacy interest was found in a person using a public phone booth, who was neither a guest nor located in a residence. 389 U.S. at 352. Thus, the facts of the particular circumstances, coupled with the overriding values and expectations of society, will determine if a victim of an unreasonable search and seizure had a right to not be searched.

This Court has also rejected the idea that a person must have a legal property interest in the premises to challenge a search. Olson, 495 U.S. at 97. Olson drew its conclusions from a similar case where the defendant challenged a search warrant used for his arrest while a guest in a friend's apartment. Jones v. United States, 362 U.S. 257, 265 (1960) (overruled on other grounds). The government claimed Jones could not challenge the search warrant because he had no legal interest in the premises where he was located. This Court held that Jones could challenge the search because he was "legitimately on the premises." Id. at 265. This Court later refined Jones' "legitimately on the premises" test as meaning "a person can have a legally sufficient interest in a place other than his own home," and the "Fourth Amendment protects him from unreasonable government intrusion into that place." Rakas v. Illinois, 439 U.S. 128, 141-142 (1978). The Fourth Amendment similarly extends to the Respondents in this case. Respondents were legitimately on the premises of their host's home because they were invited guests, and having shown a legitimate expectation of privacy while there, had a legally sufficient interest in being safe from unreasonable government intrusion.

Some students may want to get into a discussion of the overall effectiveness of each argument. Although there's nothing wrong with that, make sure to at least cover any points you want to make about dealing with negative authority.

The Minnesota v. Carter writers used an "alternate universe" method of dealing with negative authority; sometimes, however, the writer must use a direct attack. In the Miller v. Albright sample brief, the writer must deal with a case that is directly on point against him. He takes a two-pronged approach, first arguing that the test used in that case is inappropriate, advocating an alternate test. After showing how that test leads to the result he seeks, he makes an "even if" argument, showing how the "bad" test could be applied in a way that would lead to a positive result. You might **assign the Miller v. Albright brief** as part of this week's reading assignment, and discuss how it deals with the negative authority and arguments. To highlight its strengths in class, you could show the argument's outline by showing the point headings, and then focus on the writer's direct attack on negative precedent (Fiallo) by showing one or more of the brief's subsections:

I. Introduction

---

situations will demonstrate a legitimate expectation of privacy.

II.   This Court should require an "exceedingly persuasive justification" for the irrebuttable gender stereotype codified in 8 U.S.C. § 1409(a) (1994), because extreme deference to Congressional use of such gender stereotypes is unwarranted.

     A.   8 U.S.C. § 1409(a) should not escape meaningful judicial review merely because Congress acted at the height of its powers.

     B.   Even unreviewable naturalization policy choices may not be implemented by patently unconstitutional methods.

     C.   Past practices in violation of the Constitution should not be permitted to corrupt today's decisions.

III.   The use of an irrebuttable gender stereotype in 8 U.S.C. § 1409(a) is not "substantially related" to the achievement of the government's objective, and there is no "exceedingly persuasive justification" for the stereotype's use.

     A.   8 U.S.C. § 1409(a) is unconstitutionally overinclusive, and, therefore, is not "substantially related" to the achievement of the government's objective 8 U.S.C. § 1409(a).

     B.   There is no "exceedingly persuasive justification" for the use of an irrebuttable gender stereotype in 8 U.S.C. § 1409(a) because less discriminatory methods would achieve the government's objective.

IV.   8 U.S.C. § 1409(a) violates the Equal Protection Clause even under an extremely deferential level of scrutiny because congress had no "facially legitimate and bonafide" reason for using an irrebuttable gender stereotype.

Although much of the writer's analysis addresses the <u>Fiallo</u> decision, section II.A. is a good example:

     A.   8 U.S.C. § 1409(a) should not escape meaningful judicial review merely because Congress acted at the height of its powers.

The Equal Protection Clause of the Fourteenth Amendment is applicable to Congress via the Fifth Amendment. <u>See, e.g.</u>, <u>Bolling v. Sharpe</u>, 347 U.S. 497, 505 (1954). In <u>United States v. Virginia</u>, this Court held that legislation based on gender stereotypes should receive "skeptical scrutiny" upon review. 116 S. Ct. at 2275. There is no reason to use a different standard when reviewing § 1409(a) simply because it is immigration legislation.

The first reason offered by the <u>Fiallo</u> Court for its extremely deferential standard is that "'over no conceivable subject is the legislative power of Congress more complete than it is over' the admissions of aliens." Fiallo, 430 U.S. at 791 (quoting Oceanic Navigation Co. v. Stranahan, 214 U.S. 320, 339 (1909)). The quoted statement does not address the question whether Congressional power over naturalization is free from *any* meaningful judicial review; it merely points out that this power is more complete than congressional power over other areas of the law. It is a relative statement that addresses the power of Congress over naturalization by comparing that power to other powers. It wisely does not attempt to place any power of Congress about the constitution, because even when Congressional power is at its apex it may not violate the Constitution. See Marbury v. Madison, 5 U.S. (1 Cranch) 137, 180 (1803) (holding that the Constitution is the "supreme law of the land" and that only those laws made pursuant to the Constitution are to be recognized).

This Court has previously recognized that specific, Constitutional grants of authority to Congress do not allow Congress to ignore the rest of the Constitution. Almeida-Sanchez v. United States, 413 U.S. 266, 272-75 (1973). The Almeida-Sanchez Court struck down a statute that authorized searches and seizures without probable cause within "reasonable distances" from any external boundary of the United States. Id. at ???. The Court reasoned that the Naturalization Clause of the Constitution – Article I, section eight, clause four, which empowers Congress to "establish a uniform Rule of Naturalization" – did not permit Congress to enact a statute that violated the Fourth Amendment's guarantee against unreasonable searches and seizures. Id. at 272-75. Similarly, the Court refused to apply the highly deferential "rational basis" standard to a draft registration statute that exempted women, even though "judicial deference to such congressional exercise of authority is at its apogee when legislative action under the congressional authority to raise and support armies and make rules and regulations for their governance is challenged. Rostker v. Goldberg, 453 U.S. 57, 70 (1981).

This Court's holdings in Almeida-Sanchez and Rostker show that Congress is never free from meaningful judicial review. The draft registration statute that received heightened scrutiny in Rostker did not violate the Constitution because men and women were undeniably dissimilarly situated by operation of the ban on women in combat roles. 453 U.S. at ??. A skeptical scrutiny of the gender distinction in section 1409(a) will not reveal any such statutory distinction between mothers and fathers; the distinction is based on nothing more than a gender stereotype. Congress should not be permitted to dodge this scrutiny merely because it is legislating in the area of immigration.

Group exercise:

This exercise can be done as a class or within small groups. Hand out one "unit of discourse" from a brief and have students identify the parts of the formula. For example, you may wish to hand out the early version of Section I.C. of the Sarah Student brief (it is included below); another unit of discourse from a student brief in the case <u>Lebron v. Amtrak</u>[1] is also included. Depending on your students' backgrounds in legal writing and your knowledge of their particular strengths and weaknesses, you might note various aspects of the analysis in particular:

1. In each example, note that the writer mentions the client's facts in the opening paragraph, which includes the conclusion, but does not mention any client facts again until the application section.

2. In the Amtrak sample, note how the writer begins with a "rule cluster": the rule focused on, at the end of the second paragraph, is judicial gloss on another common law rule. When you ask what the rule is, many students will identify the rule articulated in the first sentence, without noticing that the *real* rule – i.e., the rule that is the focus of the analysis – occurs in the following paragraph.

3. In each example, note how each paragraph uses the phrase-that-pays at least once. This keeps the reader and the writer focused on the language at issue in that unit of discourse.

4. Note how each writer uses at least one case to illustrate behavior that *does* meet the standard of the phrase-that-pays and at least one case to illustrate behavior that *does not* meet the standard of the phrase-that-pays.

5. If you are combining discussion of chapter five and chapter six, you might discuss the effectiveness of the case descriptions and whether each case description contains the recommended elements.

6. Note the level of detail each writer provides in the application section. Why did the writer think this detail was necessary? Is this level of detail always necessary?

Of course, you can do this exercise with other parts of the sample brief or with other sample briefs. It may even be helpful to find a section in which CREXAC is not done effectively and compare it with Section I.C. or another section in which CREXAC is done effectively. E.g., section I.A. in the first sample brief is written in a very conclusory style, without much explanation. There may have been a valid reason for this decision, but you might talk to the students about how they think the lack of thorough discussion affects the effectiveness of that section of the argument.

Significant Vocabulary for Chapter Five:

Analytical formula
CREXAC

---

[1] In a nutshell, in Lebron v. Amtrak, the Court was asked to decide whether Amtrak was a state actor such that it had to respect the first amendment rights of Lebron. Lebron had contracted to rent out a billboard in Penn Station. Amtrak cancelled the contract when it saw the political content of the billboard.

Unit of Discourse
CREXAC Unit of Discourse
Phrase-that-pays
Inductive reasoning
Abstract vs. concrete

{An earlier version of Section I.C. from the <u>Minnesota v. Carter</u> petitioner's brief is reprinted below.}

Chapter Five

C. Respondents may not claim a legitimate expectation of privacy, because by engaging in criminal acts in a well-lit room, directly in front of a window facing a widely-used common area, they exhibited no subjective expectation of privacy.

Respondents, who engaged in criminal activity in an illuminated room directly in front of a window that faced a widely-used common area, manifested at most a *hope* that no one would view their unlawful acts. Respondents exhibited no actual, subjective *expectation* of privacy. Therefore, they cannot claim a legitimate expectation of privacy in Thompson's apartment and may not assert a Fourth Amendment challenge to any alleged search of the premises.

An individual seeking to establish that he possessed a legitimate expectation of privacy must first demonstrate that he possessed an "actual (subjective) expectation of privacy." Katz v. United States, 389 U.S. 347, 361 (Harlan, J., concurring). "What a person knowingly exposes to the public, even in his own home or office, is not the subject of Fourth Amendment protections." Id. at 351.

A person exhibits a subjective expectation of privacy when his conduct demonstrates his intent to keep his activity private. See id. at 352. In Katz, the defendant exhibited a subjective expectation of privacy when he closed the door to a telephone booth to prevent being overheard. Id. Katz did not knowingly expose his activity to the public; rather, his conduct demonstrated his intent to keep the activity private. Id. Therefore, the government "violated the privacy upon which he justifiably relied" when it attached an electronic surveillance device to the telephone booth. Id. Because Katz had a subjective expectation of privacy, and that expectation was one society is prepared to recognize as reasonable, he had a legitimate expectation of privacy and was entitled to assert a Fourth Amendment challenge. Id.

In contrast, when individuals in all probability know that information or activities will be revealed to others, the individuals demonstrate no actual, subjective expectation of privacy. For example, a defendant challenged the government's installation of a pen register to record his telephone calls in Smith v. Maryland, 442 U.S. 735, ??? (1979). This Court held that the defendant likely entertained no actual, subjective expectation of privacy in phone numbers he dialed, as all telephone users realize that they must convey phone numbers to the telephone company and that the telephone company records the information. Id. at ???.

Smith illustrates that even an individual who has taken cautionary measures to protect his activity from public exposure may fail to exhibit a subjective expectation of privacy if those cautionary measures are in fact inadequate to safeguard the activity from public inspection. See id. at 743. The Smith Court held that the defendant did not demonstrate an actual, subjective expectation of privacy merely by using his home phone rather than some other phone. The Court reasoned that the defendant's conduct, although perhaps "calculated to keep the contents of his conversation private," could not have preserved the privacy of the number he dialed. Id. Thus, despite what may have been some effort to maintain secrecy, the defendant exhibited no actual, subjective expectation of privacy as to the exposed information. Id. Similarly, in a 1984 decision, this Court suggested that a defendant who hid his marijuana crop from the public view with two fences may have "manifested merely a hope that no one would observe his unlawful gardening pursuits" and not an actual, subjective expectation of privacy. <u>California v. Ciraolo</u>, 476 U.S. 207, ??? (1985).

In the case at bar, Respondents' behavior and location within the apartment indicates that they had no actual, subjective expectation of privacy. Respondents manifested at most a hope that no one would observe their unlawful pursuits inside Thompson's apartment. Nothing in the record indicates Respondents took any action to preserve their privacy. Unlike the defendant in <u>Katz</u>, Respondents introduced no evidence of conduct that demonstrated an intent to keep their activity private. Though the blinds were drawn, there is no indication that Respondents drew them. <u>See</u> Record at E-2, E-10. On the night in question, Respondents were present in a first-floor apartment that had several windows at ground level. Record G-26. The windows faced a public area that apartment residents and non-residents frequented. Record G-69, G-70. As darkness fell in early evening, Respondents sat illuminated under a chandelier light at a table directly in front of one of these windows. Record G-13. Only a pane of glass and a set of blinds that featured a series of laths, Record G-50, separated Respondents from the adjacent common area. On the night in question, the blinds, though drawn, had a gap in them large enough for a citizen who passed by and an officer who stood a foot or more from the window to view easily the entire illuminated interior scene. Record G-13.

An individual in Respondents' position would have known and expected that a passer-by could look through the gaps in the blinds and see into the illuminated kitchen. Thus, Respondents could not have actually expected that their illegal activities would go unnoticed. Absent a subjective expectation, Respondents do not have a legitimate expectation of privacy and cannot assert a Fourth Amendment challenge to an alleged search of the premises. Therefore, this Court must reverse.

C. Amtrak is Not a State Actor under the Burton Test Because There is Not a Close Nexus Between the Federal Government and Gene DeAngelo's Decision not to Display Lebron's Artwork.

The third test to determine if there is state action is the "symbiotic relationship test," first developed and applied under a different name in Burton v. Wilmington Parking Authority, 365 U.S. 715, 725 (1961). Under this test, the government can be found to be a state actor if it has "so far insinuated itself into a position of interdependence with [the private entity] that it must be recognized as a joint participant in the challenged activity." Id. Because no symbiotic relationship existed between Amtrak and the federal government, Amtrak is not a state actor under the Burton test.

In refining the Burton test, the Supreme Court has indicated that a symbiotic relationship exists only when the government and the private entity are joint participants. See Jackson v. Metropolitan Edison Co., 419 U.S. 345, 357 (1974) (general state regulation of private utility does not create a "symbiotic relationship" between state and lawful termination of services). The inquiry must be whether there was a "sufficiently close nexus between the State and the challenged action of the regulated entity so that the action of the latter may be fairly treated as that of the State itself." Id. at 351.

In Burton, for example, the Court apparently found a financial close nexus between the state and a restaurant that denied service to a patron based on his race. See 365 U.S. at 723-24. The restaurant was located in a state-owned parking garage, and this Court found that the restaurant was an integral part of the State's plans, and that the garage and restaurant were interdependent. Id. The Court also found that profits the restaurant earned by excluding people based on race "not only contribute to, but are also indispensable elements in, the financial success of the government agency." Id. at 724. The Burton Court concluded that the restaurant was a state actor under the Fourteenth Amendment. Id. at 725.

General financial and regulatory ties are not sufficient to create a close nexus: the nexus must exist between the government and the challenged activity. See, e.g., Blum v. Yaretsky, 457 U.S. 991, 1004 (1982); Rendell-Baker v. Kohn, 457 U.S. 830, 832 (1982). The defendant in Rendell-Baker was a heavily state-funded and regulated school; public funds accounted for between 90-99% of the school's operating budget. Id. at 832, 840-41. The State also had the power to approve some of the school's employment decisions. Id. But when a discharged employee sued the State for wrongful termination, this Court found insufficient government involvement to constitute state action by the defendant school. Id. at 841. The Court based its decision largely on the fact that the "decisions to discharge the petitioners were not compelled or even influenced by any state regulation." Id. at 841. The lack of a close nexus between the state and the challenged action – the termination of the employees – was dispositive. See id.

The government involvement in the particular action challenged is more central to a finding of close nexus than government regulation and financial support. Blum v. Yaretsky, 457 U.S. at 1004. In Blum, several nursing home patients sued a nursing home that had decided, pursuant to state regulations, to transfer the patients to a lower-cost facility. The state had licensed the home and had paid 90% of the patients' medical expenses, but this Court found insufficient ties to the government to find state action. Id. at 1005. Despite regulations that encouraged nursing homes to transfer eligible patients to lower-cost facilities, the Court noted that the "regulations themselves do not dictate the decision to discharge or transfer in a particular case." Id. at 1010. The Blum Court decided that the mere "fact of regulation" is insufficient to demonstrate that the government is "responsible for decisions made by the entity in the course of its business." Id. at 1011. Thus, state action can be found only when a close nexus exists between the state and the particular, challenged action of the regulated entity.

Amtrak cannot be found to be a state actor because almost no nexus, let alone a close nexus, exists between the federal government and Amtrak's decision to refuse to display Lebron's work. Mr. DeAngelo, the Amtrak employee who made the decision, is not a federal employee, nor is he on Amtrak's board of directors. Congress made it a goal of Amtrak's to use its <u>own</u> "best business judgment in taking actions to minimize Federal subsidies," 45 U.S.C. § 501a(1) (1988), but neither Congress nor Amtrak's board played any part in the challenged action: the decision to deny Lebron access to the Spectacular.

Like the defendants in <u>Rendell-Baker</u> and <u>Blum</u>, Amtrak was not subject to any particular government direction in reference to the challenged action. Mr. DeAngelo made the decision alone, without reference to any government guidelines. Unlike the defendant in <u>Burton</u>, Amtrak was not making a decision that was an "indispensable element in the financial success" of the federal government when it rejected Lebron's artwork. Amtrak's decision to reject the artwork resulted in no financial benefit of any kind to the federal government.

Thus, because there was neither a financial nor a regulatory "close nexus" between the federal government and Mr. DeAngelo's decision to reject Lebron's billboard art, there is not a "symbiotic relationship" between the government and Amtrak, and Amtrak is not a state actor.

Chapter Six
Using Case Authority Effectively

Possible teaser(s) for Syllabus:

We will discuss how avoiding chocolate chip quotations will prevent Marie Antoinette syndrome [Section 6.2.1], and how Katie Couric introductions will discourage readers from skipping chunky quotes [Section 6.2.2]. You should also be prepared to distinguish authorities from sources [Section 6.5.2] and rule authorities from illustrative authorities [Section 6.1]. Identify someone who likes to be interrupted in the middle of a sentence [Section 6.5.3]. All students should be able to list the elements needed in an effective case description [Section 6.1]

Teaching Goals

How to deal with negative authorities
How to write effective case descriptions
How to use quotations effectively
How to analogize and distinguish cases effectively

Changes from Second Edition:

As noted above, the discussion of how to address an opponent's authorities has been moved from Chapter 6 to Chapter 5. Accordingly, teachers should note that the subsections within Chapter 6 will have different enumeration than in past editions. Chapter 6 also includes a new sub-section within the section on case descriptions: Accuracy in Case Descriptions. This section gives advice on how to avoid common problems in mischaracterizing cases. The section on Tom Brokaw Introductions has been changed to Katie Couric Introductions. The section on unpublished decisions has been updated and notes that these decisions are often referred to as "nonprecedential" decisions

Audio-visual aids:

A powerpoint addresses effective case descriptions and effective topic sentences within case descriptions. This powerpoint could be used in 2 pieces, in 2 separate sessions, or it could be used after the concept of the "template" has been introduced (in chapter 10).

Pre-class homework to assign in addition to the readings:

If you are going to ask students to work on case descriptions, you might ask all students to bring a description of a particular case to class. Ideally, you should assign a case that all students should be citing in their briefs. You can ask the students to pair up with people on the same side to write case descriptions; the differences between petitioner's and respondent's descriptions of the same case, for example, could provide fodder for class discussion.

Ideas for Lecture/Discussion/Demonstration:

Chapter Six addresses many of the common problems that students have when using case

111

authority in legal argument. If your class time is limited, you may wish to forgo discussion of this chapter, or to combine it with your discussion of Chapter Five and allude to it as needed. In the alternative, you may assign it before the macro draft is turned in, but discuss it after, with reference to the most common problems that your students exhibited.

The text gives examples of all or most of the concepts addressed in the chapter. This teacher's manual will recommend alternate examples for some of the concepts that may be used as a handout or an overhead. Of course, you may wish to create overheads from the text to use as a backdrop for discussion, even if you don't go painstakingly through each example.

To illustrate the concept of authorities v. sources, I create two overheads of the same point, followed by the same citation to a (usually fictional) sixth circuit court case. I tell the students that I am going to show them excerpts from two different briefs, and they have to tell me the difference between the two excerpts. The students squint, looking at everything from punctuation to spacing. I finally put both on together, and tell them that the language and the citations are identical. I do some Socratic questioning, reminding them that the excerpts are from two different briefs. Eventually, I tell them that this is a trick question, and ask, "what's the difference between these two excerpts? [pause] What's a good answer to any question in law school?" The students say "it depends," and then I say, "what does it depend on?" And we work from there. The "correct" answer is that it depends on the court that each brief-writer is writing to. If you are writing to a sixth circuit court, or to a district court within the sixth circuit, citing to a sixth circuit decision is perfectly appropriate. If you are writing to the U.S. Supreme Court, or to a court in another jurisdiction, this citation is merely a citation to a source.

Case Descriptions:

While the text discussing case descriptions is fairly self-explanatory, you may want to put further illustrations on an overhead for class discussion. The examples below consist of bad and good examples based on a Knowles v. Iowa brief.

This set of three starts with the worst and works up to the best:

Concerns over officer safety are enough to justify a search incident to arrest even in situation in which the arresting officer had no subjective fear of the defendant and did not need to conduct the search for evidentiary reasons. United States v. Robinson, 414 U.S. 218, 234, 236 (1973). Robinson dealt with an arrest for driving with a revoked permit. In fact, the officer arrested the defendant for two violations, both related to the validity of his driver's license. The Court examined the question whether a police officer was justified in searching a crumpled cigarette package, even though he knew that the package did not contain a weapon and even though he already had sufficient evidence for the arrest. 414 U.S. at 223.

Concerns over officer safety are enough to justify a search incident to arrest even in situation in which the arresting officer had no subjective fear of the defendant and did not need to conduct the search for evidentiary reasons. United States v. Robinson, 414 U.S. 218, 234, 236 (1973). In Robinson, the arresting officer was in the course of arresting the defendant for two violations related to the validity of his driver's license. Id. at 223. While searching the defendant's person, the officer discovered a crumpled cigarette package. Id. Although the officer had no further evidence to gather for the crime of driving with a revoked permit, and although the officer knew that the cigarette package did not contain a weapon, the officer searched the crumpled package and discovered a quantity of heroin. Id.

Concerns over officer safety are enough to justify a search incident to arrest even in situation in which the arresting officer had no subjective fear of the defendant and did not need to conduct the search for evidentiary reasons. United States v. Robinson, 414 U.S. 218, 234, 236 (1973). In Robinson, the Court refused to suppress heroin discovered in a crumpled cigarette package during a search of the defendant's person after a traffic arrest. Id. at 223. The officer needed no more evidence to justify the defendant's arrest for driving without a license, and he admitted that he did not believe that the crumpled package contained a weapon. Id.

Note that the writer did not begin discussing the reasoning until the second paragraph because the facts were so significant to the argument. The reasoning follows:

In finding the search legal, the Court first noted that the reason for the authority to search incident to a lawful arrest depended just as much on the need to disarm the suspect as it did on the need to preserve evidence. Id. at 234. The Court noted that a search incident to arrest could be justified purely by concerns over officer safety – despite the fact that a need to preserve evidence did not exist in that situation. Id. The Court observed that a person arrested for driving with a revoked license is just as likely to possess dangerous weapons as a person arrested for other crimes. Id.

If you discuss these examples in class, you can point out (or have students point out) the various elements of issue, disposition, facts, and reasoning. Note that it's not necessarily wrong to have a lengthy case description, but it is wrong to waste words in a case description.

Effective Parentheticals:

Again, if you wish to review this concept in class, you might ask the students to try to identify the four elements in the parentheticals below. Although some effective parentheticals do not have all four elements, it's usually better to err on the side of including information. The only exception to this guideline might be in an introductory section or paragraph, when the case will be described in more depth a paragraph or two later. The first example below does not tell the reader what the court was looking at when it made the statement about officer safety. The second example does not provide all of the details that a textual description would, but it provides sufficient context for the quotation and gives the reader an accurate picture of the situation as one *not* involving an apparent threat of harm to the officer.

☹   See also Washington v. Chrisman, 455 U.S. 1, 7 (1982) (noting that "every arrest must be presumed to present a risk of danger to the arresting officer").

☺   See also Washington v. Chrisman, 455 U.S. 1, 7 (1982) (officer who conducted a plain view search after following arrested defendant to his room to retrieve identification acted properly because "every arrest must be presumed to present a risk of danger to the arresting officer").

Ideas for Group Work/Exercises:

A particularly effective group exercise is to ask the students to **bring a copy of a significant case that you expect both petitioners and respondents to use in the brief.** Divide the class into petitioner and respondent groups. At the very least, you can have petitioners and respondents each describe the case from their point of view. If you have more groups, you could have some groups write a textual description and others write a parenthetical description. If the case is relevant to more than one sub-issue, different groups could write a parenthetical description that would be appropriate to different sub-issues.

When the students share their case descriptions, note whether they used language efficiently, focused on the phrase-that-pays, and included all of the needed elements (for this exercise, you might presume that all elements are needed). Note the differences between petitioners' and respondents' descriptions, and ask whether each has described the law accurately. Note how different details may be relevant depending on which issue the writer is using the case to illustrate.

If group work is impractical, you may wish to **assign students to turn in a textual and/or parenthetical one day before the class meeting.** If you ask students to send this to you via e-mail, you can block and copy (and edit) the examples to provide fodder for class discussion.

Significant Vocabulary Words in Chapter Six:

Marie Antoinette Syndrome
Katie Couric Introductions
Chocolate Chip quotations
Rule Authority v. Illustrative Authority
Authority v. source
string citation

Chapter Seven
Seeing What You Have Written: The Self-Graded Draft

Possible Teaser(s) for Syllabus:
Learn how using highlighters can help you avoid an "eclipse of the brain." (Section 7.1.1).

Learning Goals of Class Meeting:
How to use the self-graded draft
By doing a self-grading of someone else's document, help students see the benefits of good analysis and/or the problems of weak analysis.

Changes from Second Edition:

No significant changes.

Pre-class assignment other than the readings:

The students' first turned-in draft is due the day before this class meeting. I ask them to bring pink, green, blue, and yellow highlighters to the class meeting. I usually bring extra highlighters that I lend to students who need them, and I usually get most of them back.

Audio-visual aids:

The website contains a powerpoint and word processing files to use in teaching this exercise. At the end of this section of the teachers' manual, you will find materials that can be made into handouts.

Ideas for Lecture and Discussion:
In this class, my first task is convincing the students that they need this exercise. I do this by showing them that sometimes their eyes see things that aren't there, or *don't* see things that are there. This exercise came from a long-forgotten e-mail, and it was not presented as an in-class exercise – just a fun trick. I thank my niece, Lisa Beazley, who first sent it to me. I put the sentence below up on the overhead (it is in the powerpoint), *exactly* as it appears below. I tell the students that it is a reading test, and ask them to see how quickly they can tell me how many times the letter "F" appears in the sentence. (Stop now and see how many times it appears; I fell completely for the trick the first time I read it.)

**FINISHED FILES ARE THE RE-
SULT OF YEARS OF SCIENTIF-
IC STUDY COMBINED WITH
THE EXPERIENCE OF YEARS.**

Most people see three "F's." Actually, there are six of them. Apparently because the letter "F" is pronounced as a "V" sound in the word "of" (which appears three times), many people don't process it as an "F." In class, I put the sentence up on an overhead. I enlarge it to 30-point type, but I keep the layout identical to the layout I first saw (hyphenating in the same places, using capital letters, etc.) for fear of ruining the trick

As soon as the sentence is up on the overhead, I start asking the class, "How many think the letter "F" appears only once?" raising my hand to show that I want them to raise theirs. "How many think only twice?" Then, knowing the reluctance of students to raise their hands for this kind of exercise, I make my voice sound disappointed, as if they have beaten me, and ask, "How many think it appears only three times." (I use such disappointment in my voice that I don't even give the inflection of a question mark.) In my class of 50-60 students, a large number of hands shoot up, and I announce: "it appears six times." It's always fun to watch the stunned expressions, including those on the faces of many students who agreed that there were three F's but did not raise their hands. Before going on, I have found, I must stop and point out all the "F's," unless I want students pointing and whispering and nodding as they try to find them all. (The powerpoint contains this exercise, including a slide with all of the F's underlined.)

At this point, I segue to a discussion of the "eclipse of the brain" phenomenon discussed in the chapter, and explain that a brain eclipse makes it harder for them to revise their own writing, because they think everything's in there, in the brief, when really some of it may still be inside their heads. Because the readings make this point clear, I don't belabor it. I try to make them realize that I know how hard it is to write and revise their own work, particularly when their short term memory is telling them, "it's fine, it's fine, go to bed!"

Ideas for Group Work/Exercises:

For this exercise I first distribute 1) the self-grading guidelines and 2) a unit of discourse from a student brief. I ask the students to work through seven of the eight of the self-grading tasks, showing each stage of the exercise on the screen after the students have completed it. I find that completing the tasks helps students to see how each works and to flush out any questions.[3]

Although I use an overhead projector for nearly all of my exercises, for this exercise I use a laptop and an LCD projector – I find that this is the best way to put color up on the screen. I use several handouts that are available on the website. They include:

1. Self-grading guidelines (short)
2. Self-grading guidelines (long)
3. "Amtrak" handout
4. Robinette handout #1
5. Robinette handout #2 (revised)

---

[3] **Note:** You may have some students who are color-blind; if you do, you can recommend that they identify four different methods of marking the text. For example, they could draw a box around the "phrases-that-pay," underline citations, highlight their client's facts (because using one color would not be a problem) and put slash marks on either side of their connection-conclusions. As long as they provide a "key" on the paper for the teacher who will be reviewing their work, they should have no problem completing the exercise.

The website will contain several versions of the the Amtrak handout. First as a "clean" or "blank" handout, and also with each stage of self-grading recorded, so that you can show the students what their papers should look like. The website also shows the Robinette handout as a blank and with the self-grading completed. Because powerpoints are so limited in the amount of text that can appear on a screen, for this exercise I move back and forth between a powerpoint and word processing files. I find that WordPerfect works best for this exercise. If you cannot use WordPerfect, the better option is to print out the materials in color (or do the highlighting by hand) and then show them on a document camera.

Using the powerpoint, I do the "finding F" exercise and explain concepts about the self-grading process. Then the students self-grade the Amtrak handout, step by step, and I move to the word processing files after about every second step to show the students what their documents should look like. The Amtrak handout is very easy to self-grade; all of the pieces are in place. By taking them through all of the steps, I try to flush out any misunderstandings about the process.

As you go through each task, you might want to spend time talking about what they should be thinking about when they self-grade their own work. You can use the self-grading guidelines, which give suggestions, as a starting point. For example, when they are looking for the explanation section, you might talk to them about looking for effective case descriptions, or about evaluating the types of authorities that they cited.

After each set of tasks is completed, I show them approximately how it should look by showing two pages at a time on the screen. (This is possible with WordPerfect software currently; it may not be possible with other types of software. If it is not possible, you may wish to hold up two hard copy pages at a time.) Thus, I start by showing them the "blank" (unannotated) copy, then I show them the "Focus" copy after they have completed tasks 1 & 2, the "Explanation" copy after they have completed tasks 3 & 4, and so on. You will note that the website and the Teacher's Manual contains a sample focus list that you can show them after step 8.

Showing two pages at a time is the best way to make the pattern of colors clear: The initial paragraph(s) in a unit of discourse may contain three of the colors because the writer may articulate the rule, which includes the phrase-that-pays (pink), cite to authority for that rule (green), and state in a conclusory way what happens when that rule is applied to the facts (blue).

In a well-written unit of discourse, the paragraph(s) in which the writer articulates the rule should be followed by one or more paragraphs that contain only pink and green highlights, as the writer explains how one or more courts have interpreted the phrase-that-pays, citing to authority as she goes. When the application begins, we should see pink and blue, as the writer says "phrase-that-pays equals (or doesn't equal) my facts." The application may or may not include green highlights, depending on whether the writer analogized or distinguished her case facts from those of authority cases. Finally, the students will see yellow highlights, when the writer articulated a connection-conclusion and, ideally, tied this unit of discourse to other relevant aspects of the argument.

The sudden appearance of the blue highlights after numerous paragraphs of pink and green is mildly dramatic, and you might want to use this reality (in the Amtrak unit of discourse) to emphasize the importance of finishing their explanation sections *before* applying law to facts. In the Robinette unit of discourse, in contrast, the pattern does not emerge so neatly.

I take care to stress that the color alone is not what indicates a good brief, although certain color patterns are *consistent* with good briefs. For example, a brief that used its explanation section to simply reiterate the holdings of the authority cases would have the "good" color pattern because it would have pink (phrase that pays) and green (citations), but would probably not contain effective explanation sections because the writer would not say how the courts had applied the phrase that pays to the facts of those cases. The colors and the marginal labels merely tell the writer (and the teacher) where to look for certain elements. The placement of certain elements can be significant (e.g., if the application comes before the explanation), but the substance of those elements is also significant.

After the Amtrak handout is completed, I distribute the Robinette handout #1, and display a powerpoint screen that lists all of the steps. I have the students complete the self-grading for this task on their own. I remind them that if they have any trouble (and they will), they might first complete the objective tasks (highlighting client facts, highlighting citations) as a way to help them with the subjective tasks.

This handout is much more difficult to self grade; after they finish, I have a class discussion and talk to them about it. Most students will find a focus and then discover that the phrase-that-pays disappears early in the section. Some students will find that the writer actually has two focuses. There is a second phrase-that-pays, but even that is a less effective phrase-that-pays than it could be. With some Socratic questioning, I help them identify a better phrase-that-pays, and then I distribute an improved version of the draft. I find that this part of the exercise is very helpful, and I tell students that they should expect problems of this type in their own writing – the problems here are some of the exact problems that self-grading is meant to find. The Robinette handout #2 shows an attempt at revision; the unit of discourse is broken into two subparts. If you have time, you could have the students self-grade this as well. In my class, I usually just show them a completed self-grading of the document, pointing out how the writer could have made changes to improve the focus and persuasiveness of the analysis. This second example is far from perfect, and is meant to represent how a student might complete a "quick and dirty" revision prior to meeting with the teacher for a conference.

You may have sample briefs or excerpts that you would like to use. Although some of the website handouts may have a special column created for the marginal notes, I never require my students to create such a column, nor do I expect them to create a computer document highlighting these features. I think this exercise is much easier to do with highlighter and hard copy in hand, even for our computer-loving students.

Two sets of self-grading guidelines appear below, suitable for handouts. One is more simple, and the other is more detailed, with suggested solutions to anticipated problems. In recent years, I have posted the "detailed guidelines" on the course webpage and distributed only the more straightforward guidelines. You may wish to use them as is, or you may wish to develop your own self-grading guidelines (*See* Mary Beth Beazley, *The Self-Graded Draft: Teaching Students to Revise Using Guided Self-Critique*, 3 Legal Writing 175 (1997), for ideas on developing guidelines).

Using the Self-Graded Draft When Critiquing:

It is entirely possible for self-grading and teacher critiques to co-exist. I have talked to some colleagues who require that students self-grade every exercise before they hand it in. The teachers can then use the students' critiques as they fashion their own. For at least one draft, however, I think the self-grading can *almost* substitute for the teacher's critique. In a three-draft course, I have the students self-grade the first (macro) draft, and I tell them that I will not be doing an in-depth critique – the self-grading will be the in-depth critique. I read each draft, I answer the questions on the criteria sheet, I fill in the final comment page and check the appropriate slots, *and* I answer their private memo questions (I strongly encourage private memo questions for this reason, and I make clear that they can use private memos to ask for more in-depth critiques). Before or after I have read all of the macro drafts, I come up with a list of authorities that I see as a minimum for each side, and a brief outline for each side of the case.

They must come to the conference with the self-grading, a focus list, and a final comment. Based on my review (with *no* comments on the body of the document), I am ready for them, with certain concerns that I know I want to discuss. First, though, I look at their "focus list." The focus list tells me a) about their coverage – what issues did they address? and b) about their large-scale organization – did they address the issues in an appropriate order? I discuss these two points as needed. I then look at the self-graded draft, noting only the green highlights (authority). These tell me about their research. I compare their research with my list, again, talking to them as needed. Although I don't expect that the students will have identical lists of authorities, there are usually some authorities that are a minimum requirement for each side. If any of those are missing, or if they have little else beyond the minimum, we talk about research process.

The third step in the conference is to look at their legal analysis. Based on my reading, I may have spotted certain sections that I think are stronger or weaker. I may direct them, "let's take a look at your I.B. section" (if time is short), or, if there is more time, I may ask, "which section do you think has the best analysis? Which section(s) were you worried about after doing the self-grading?" If I see "chunks of blue syndrome" (where they apply the law to the facts before explaining the rule) or "ping-pong syndrome" (going back and forth between explanation and application -- usually because they are applying cases rather than rules), I can zero in on that and discuss it. In the alternative, I can look for sections that follow the color scheme, and zero in on certain aspects, looking to see if the explanation is thorough, or if the application of law to facts takes the opponent's angle into account. At the end of the conference, I look at their "final comment" to see if I have anything to add as they plan their revision.

This method took me a while to get used to. At first, it was almost painful for me *not* to do detailed critiques of the macro drafts. Now, however, I love the method, because it keeps us all focused on the big-picture issues of content and large-scale organization, research, and analysis. I don't get into roadmaps or topic sentences or a variety of other minutiae, and they aren't distracted from substance by questions about citation form. The draft is a break for me because it is certainly easier to read and react than to read and critique. The method allows the students one draft where the focus is only on substance. In the second (micro) draft, I do complete a detailed critique, and then hold a conference, and thus I think they have the benefits of both the self-grading and my critique – just on different drafts. I think it's perfectly appropriate to require self-grading for the micro draft – you might even add or substitute other elements that you care particularly about (e.g., have them highlight different elements of the case descriptions in different colors, have them highlight the places where they deal with the opponent's argument/authorities in a different color) at that stage of the process.

Significant vocabulary for Chapter Seven:
"brain eclipse"
unit of discourse

Appellate Advocacy

Self-grading

To be completed before the conference on the draft of the brief.

Before you begin to self-grade: You will need: 1) Four highlighters: Pink, Green, Blue, and Yellow; 2) One hard copy of your draft; 3) a place to write and take notes (e.g., laptop). **After completing each step below, note any private memo questions for your adjunct.** If you are having trouble with any particular step, consult the "detailed guidelines" on the course TWEN site.

1. Identify the Focus of Each Unit of Discourse: First, identify how many "CREXAC units of discourse" you have in your argument section. (*See* the text, pp. 61-63.) Within each CREXAC unit of discourse, write "focus" in the margin next to the first sentence(s) that contain(s) the rule, policy, assertion or other thesis that is the focus of that unit of discourse. Do *not* write "focus" next to every statement that could be called a rule. If you cannot find a clearly-articulated focus for any unit of discourse, you may want to draft one now, in the margin or in your notes.

2. Highlight Phrase-That-Pays in Pink: Within the sentence that articulates each focus, identify the key terms, or "phrase-that-pays" ("PTP"). Highlight each PTP in **pink** *wherever it appears within its unit of discourse.* Each unit of discourse will probably have a different phrase-that-pays.

3. Highlight Citations to Cases, Statutes, etc. in Green: Highlight each citation (whether long-form, short form, or Id.) in **green.** Do *not* highlight citations to your case's facts, even if those facts appeared in the decisions below, and thus have formal citations. Highlight citations only (i.e., do *not* highlight quoted language.

4. Identify the Explanation of your Rule/Focus: Write the word "Explanation" in the margin next to the paragraphs in which you *explained* the rule/focus. Generally, you will have one or more paragraphs containing only pink and green highlights, because in those paragraphs, you will be explaining the meaning of the PTP according to various authorities. Do not presume that all paragraphs with pink and green highlights are explanation paragraphs.

5. Highlight Your Case's Facts in Blue: Throughout the entire argument section, highlight any references to *your case's* facts in **blue.** (Remember, if the language of enacted law is at issue, that language may sometimes act as your "facts.")

6. Identify the Application of Law to Facts: Within each point heading section and sub-section, write "Application" in the margin next to the sentences in which you discuss how the rule/focus for that section applies or does not apply to those facts. Look for paragraphs with both pink highlights (PTP) and blue highlights (client facts) when looking for application, but do not presume that every paragraph with pink and blue highlights is an application paragraph. Similarly, **some paragraphs may contain both explanation and application**; do not presume that a paragraph has no "application" simply because it has already been labeled with "explanation."

7. Identify and Highlight in Yellow the Connection-Conclusions that end each Unit of Discourse: Within each unit of discourse, write "C-C" in the margin next to the sentence in which you explicitly state your "Connection-Conclusion" that is, your conclusion for that unit of discourse. Highlight the connection-conclusion in **yellow.** Do *not* highlight any statement that could be characterized as a conclusion (particularly, do not highlight the conclusion at the beginning of the

Chapter Seven

sub-section). In the Connection-Conclusion, you should make explicit how the analysis of this issue or sub-issue *connects* to the point you have made in this section and, if appropriate, to your overall analysis. **<u>Note that your Connection-Conclusion may appear in a paragraph that also contains application.</u>**

8. <u>Create a Separate Focus List</u>: Repeat Steps 1-7 for each CREXAC unit of discourse. After you have done so, type or block and copy the"focus" for each CREXAC unit of discourse (identified in Step 1) into a separate document in which you list each focus in order of appearance. You and your adjunct can use this list to review your issues and discuss your large-scale organization.

9. <u>Write a Final Comment</u>: By now, you should have an idea of some of the areas you want to concentrate on in your revision. List the two or three most important elements or sections that you plan to revise. You may also want to note the aspects of your brief that you believe are strongest.

IN YOUR CONFERENCE, your adjunct will expect you to have three things: (1) the highlighted and annotated draft, (2) the focus list, and (3) the final comment. You should be able to discuss what you did in the brief and why. Your comments and the self-grading will be in an important part of the conference. The best way to prepare for the conference is to complete the self-grading and to begin revisions that the self-grading reveals a need for. *Do not presume that you must wait for the conference to begin revising your brief.*

To be completed before the conference on the MACRO draft of the brief.

Before you begin to self-grade: You will need: **(1)** Four highlighters: Pink, Blue, Yellow, and Green; **(2)** One hard copy of your macro draft; **(3)** A place to write and take notes (e.g., laptop). **As you complete each step below, note any private memo questions for your adjunct.**

1. Identify Rule/Focus in Each Unit of Discourse: First, identify how many "CREXAC units of discourse" you have in your argument section. (*See* the text, pp. 61-63.) Within each CREXAC unit of discourse, write "focus" in the margin next to the first sentence(s) that contain(s) the rule, policy, assertion, or other thesis <u>that is the focus</u> of that unit of discourse. Do *not* write "focus" next to every statement that could be called a rule. If you find that you cannot find a clearly-articulated focus for any unit of discourse, you may want to draft one now.

Common Concerns:
*Frequently, writers at this stage have failed to articulate the point that they are focusing on in some sections of the document. (In legal arguments, the point they are focusing on is usually a rule.) If you find that you have not articulated the focus of any section of your argument, write that focus in the margin – whether the focus is a rule, a policy, an assertion, or some other thesis. Remember, even if the rule is implicit in all of the support you've cited or discussed, most readers need an <u>explicit</u> articulation of the rule that governs the issue, and they like the rule to come <u>early</u> in the analysis of the issue. If the unit of discourse is focused on introductory material or historical analysis (talk to your adjunct about whether such a section is appropriate for your case), label as your "focus" the thesis of that section: e.g., what point are you trying to make about the history of the rule, statute, or amendment? Have you articulated that point early in the discussion?

*If you are "creating" or "finding" a rule through inductive reasoning, you should still articulate the rule early in the section. Follow your articulation of the rule with an explanation of where it came from and/or how that "rule" has been applied in the past (even if the courts who decided the cases you cite for support didn't label the rule in the same way as you have labeled it here).

2. Highlight Phrase-That-Pays in Pink: Within the sentence that articulates each focus, identify the "phrase-that-pays" and highlight each phrase-that-pays in **pink** *wherever it appears within its unit of discourse.* Each unit of discourse will probably have a different phrase-that-pays.

Common Concerns:
*Hint for identifying the phrase-that-pays: Presume that each rule/focus *does* have a phrase-that-pays. You can often find the phrase-that-pays by identifying what you are trying to prove. To do this, **(1)** mentally restate the rule as an if-then proposition (Don't presume that rules should be stated as if-then statements in the document itself), then **(2)** look in the "if" clause to identify what you are trying to prove. That thing that you are proving usually constitutes the main "phrase-that-pays."

       An "if-then" rule says, e.g., "if phrase-that-pays exists, then Result occurs." Your analysis of that rule would try to explain what the phrase-that-pays means so that you could predict whether the phrase-that-pays exists in your client's case. Once you know whether the phrase-that-pays exists, you would know whether Result would occur.
EXAMPLE OF RULE AS WRITTEN IN BRIEF: A gender-based distinction can survive intermediate scrutiny only if it is substantially related to the government's important objective.

EXAMPLE OF SAME RULE STATED AS AN IF-THEN CLAUSE: **IF** a gender-based distinction is substantially related to an important governmental objective, **THEN** it can survive intermediate scrutiny.

This writer is trying to prove whether or not the gender-based distinction in the client's case is "substantially related to an important governmental objective." Thus, "substantially related to an important governmental objective" is the phrase-that-pays, and that phrase (or any words from that phrase) should be highlighted wherever they appear in that section. Of course, the phrase-that-pays can also be affected by how courts interpret rules and their components. If courts had separately analyzed "substantially related" and "important governmental objective," then it's possible that the writer could have two phrases-that-pay here, and should have one point heading section for each. Note that sometimes self-grading will reveal that you need to break an argument into two parts.

3. Highlight Citations to Cases, Statutes, etc. in Green: Highlight each support citation (or reference to cases, statutes, etc., even if not in a formal citation) in **green.** Do *not* highlight citations to client facts, even if those facts appeared in the decisions below, and thus have formal citations. Highlight citations only; do not highlight quoted language from cited sources.

Common Concerns:
*First, note *how many different* citations you have. At a bare minimum, you should cite to one authority or source for each rule. Generally, the more abstract/controversial the rule is, the more explanation (and thus the more support) you need to provide; the more concrete/non-controversial the rule is, the more often you can get away with citing one case with a parenthetical. Ideally, you will have cited at least one authority or source which makes clear what the rule or policy *does* mean and at least one authority or source which makes clear what the rule or policy *does not* mean. Using this method helps the reader understand the "boundaries" of the rule – that is, what situations it does and does not apply to.

*Second, note *what type* of citations you have. Most or ideally, all, of your "rule support " (support cited to support a rule) should be from mandatory authorities. Some of your "explanatory support" (support cited to explain or illustrate how rules have been applied in the past) can be non-mandatory cases, but a lower court case should almost always be cited in the context of a mandatory rule or policy that the non-mandatory court case is illustrating.

*Third, note *how much analysis* of your support you've provided. For example, for a case that illustrates an abstract, controversial rule, you may need to provide a lengthier, in-text case analysis (addressing the legally significant issue, disposition, facts, and reasoning), while for a case illustrating a non-controversial point, or for a secondary case illustrating a controversial point, a parenthetical case description may be adequate.

*Not every reference to a case or statute means you are citing that resource as support for a legal proposition. Sometimes, for example, when you are saying that a canon of construction should be applied to the language of the statute in a certain way, the language of that statute is a fact.

4. Identify the Explanation of your Rule/Focus: Write the word "Explanation" in the margin next to the paragraphs in which you *explained* the rule/focus. Generally, you will have one or more paragraphs containing only pink and green highlights, because in those paragraphs, you will be explaining the meaning of the phrase-that-pays, according to various authorities. Do not presume that all paragraphs with pink and green highlights are explanation paragraphs.

Common Concerns:

*Generally, the more abstract and controversial the language or rule at issue is, the more explanation you need to provide for the reader. Explanation often consists of discussions of cases in which the rule has been applied in the past. Thus, if your rule is abstract and/or controversial, the phrase-that-pays should appear frequently, because you should be telling the reader, e.g., "In <u>case</u>, the Court held that phrase-that-pays included [X behavior] . . . . The court reasoned that . . ." "In <u>other case</u>, the Court noted that phrase-that-pays did not include [Q behavior] . . . . because [reasoning]. . . ."

*If your explanation is short, and/or the phrase-that-pays appears infrequently, scrutinize your analysis to decide whether a) the language is not controversial and thus little explanation is needed (if this is true, no revision is necessary), b) explanation is needed, but it is not included (if this is true, you need to do more research, include more analysis, or both), or c) explanation is included, but the explanation is not as clear as it could be because you (or the court) used language other than the phrase-that-pays. If this last one is true, adding language connecting the case analysis to the phrase-that-pays should make your analysis clearer for the reader. For example, you could say, "The court apparently believed that [phrase-that-pays existed], because it found [or stated, noted, held, etc.]. . . . .

*If your opponent would explain this rule using different cases – i.e., because you disagree about what the rule means – you should try to contradict that explanation, either directly or indirectly. For example, you might cite one or more of the cases your opponent would cite and contradict his or her analysis, e.g., "While it is true that in [X case] the court held [Y], that case is not relevant here [or was wrongly decided, or has been implicitly overruled . . .]

5. Highlight Your Case's Facts in Blue: Throughout the entire argument section, highlight any references to *your case's* facts in **blue.** (Remember, if the language of enacted law is at issue, that language may sometimes act as your "facts.")

6. Identify the Application of Law to Facts: Within each point heading section and sub-section, write "Application" in the margin next to the sentences in which you discuss how the rule/focus for that section applies or does not apply to those facts. Look for paragraphs with both pink highlights (phrase-that-pays) and blue highlights (client facts) when looking for application, but do not presume that every paragraph with pink and blue highlights is an application paragraph. Similarly, **some paragraphs may contain both explanation and application**; do not presume that a paragraph has no "application" simply because it has already been labeled with "explanation."

Common Concerns:

*Have you explicitly applied the rule to the facts of your client's case? Do the blue and pink markings appear close together? (I.e., at some point you should be saying, "Phrase-that-pays equals or does not equal client's facts because . . . .") Have you "milked" your application when needed by explaining how the facts in this case meet or do not meet the standard? For abstract and/or controversial rules, have you analogized your case to or distinguished it from illustrative support cases? If your opponent would argue that the rule applies in a different way, have you contradicted that analysis, either directly or indirectly?

7. Identify and Highlight in Yellow the Connection-Conclusions that end each Unit of Discourse: Within each unit of discourse, write "C-C" in the margin next to the sentence in which you explicitly state your "Connection-Conclusion" that is, your conclusion for that unit of discourse.

Highlight the connection-conclusion in **yellow**. Do *not* highlight any statement that could be characterized as a conclusion (particularly, do not highlight the conclusion at the beginning of the sub-section). In the Connection-Conclusion, you should make explicit how the analysis of this issue or sub-issue *connects* to the point you have made in this section and, if appropriate, to your overall analysis. **Note that your Connection-Conclusion may appear in a paragraph that also contains application.**

Common Concerns:

*Often, the connection-conclusion for a sub-section will clarify the connection between that sub-section and the main point heading (e.g., "because there is no close nexus, Amtrak is not a state actor"); similarly, the connection-conclusion for a roman heading will clarify the connection between the roman heading and the writer's ultimate argument (e.g., "because Amtrak is not a state actor, Lebron's first amendment rights were not violated, and this Court should affirm the decision below").

*Note that an effective connection-conclusion will usually include any phrases-that-pay discussed in the section or sub-section. *Don't worry about being too obvious.* Your reader will appreciate the sense of closure that you provide by saying, in essence, "now I'm done talking about this issue or sub-issue." Note: Do *not* simply highlight the last sentence in the point heading section or sub-section. Read the sentences in the last paragraph, and see if you have actually articulated a connection-conclusion. If you have not, write a connection-conclusion in the margin.

8. Create a Separate Focus List: Repeat Steps 1-7 for each CREXAC unit of discourse. After you have done so, block and copy the "focus" for each CREXAC unit of discourse (identified in Step 1) into a separate document in which you list each focus in order of appearance. You and your adjunct can use this list to review your issues and discuss your large-scale organization.

9. Write a Final Comment: By now, you should have an idea of some of the areas you want to concentrate on in your revision. If you are unsure, review the "Common Concerns" listed under some of the tasks in the handout on the website. List the two or three most important elements or sections that you plan to revise. You may also want to note the areas of your brief that you believe are strongest.

IN YOUR CONFERENCE, your teacher will expect you to have three things: **(1)** the highlighted and annotated draft, **(2)** the focus list, and **(3)** the final comment. You should be able to discuss what you did in the brief and why. Remember that, although your adjunct will have read your brief, he or she will usually not have a written critique. The critique will come through your discussion in the conference. In most conferences, you and your adjunct will first address the document's content and large-scale organization (by reviewing your focus list) and then address your research (by reviewing your green-highlighted citations). These two items will usually be followed by a discussion of your legal analysis (by reviewing particular sections within the brief). Some adjuncts may wish to start the conference with a discussion of your private memo questions, while others will save that discussion for the end, and still others may give you answers in writing instead of spending time in the conference.

The best way to prepare for the conference is to complete the self-grading and to begin any revisions that the self-grading reveals a need for. *Do not presume that you must wait for the conference to begin revision work on your brief.*

C.   Amtrak is Not a State Actor under the Burton Test Because There is Not a Close Nexus Between the Federal Government and Gene DeAngelo's Decision not to Display Lebron's Artwork.

The third test to determine if there is state action is the "symbiotic relationship test," first developed and applied under a different name in Burton v. Wilmington Parking Authority, 365 U.S. 715, 725 (1961). Under this test, the government can be found to be a state actor if it has "so far insinuated itself into a position of interdependence with [the private entity] that it must be recognized as a joint participant in the challenged activity." Id. Because no symbiotic relationship existed between Amtrak and the federal government, Amtrak is not a state actor under the Burton test.

In refining the Burton test, the Supreme Court has indicated that a symbiotic relationship exists only when the government and the private entity are joint participants. See Jackson v. Metropolitan Edison Co., 419 U.S. 345, 357 (1974) (general state regulation of private utility does not create a "symbiotic relationship" between state and lawful termination of services). The inquiry must be whether there was a "sufficiently close nexus between the State and the challenged action of the regulated entity so that the action of the latter may be fairly treated as that of the State itself." Id. at 351.

In Burton, for example, the Court apparently found a financial close nexus between the state and a restaurant that denied service to a patron based on his race. See 365 U.S. at 723-24. The restaurant was located in a state-owned parking garage, and this Court found that the restaurant was an integral part of the State's plans, and that the garage and restaurant were interdependent. Id. The Court also found that profits the restaurant earned by excluding people based on race "not only contribute to, but are also indispensable elements in, the financial success of the government agency." Id. at 724. The Burton Court concluded that the restaurant was a state actor under the Fourteenth Amendment. Id. at 725.

General financial and regulatory ties are not sufficient to create a close nexus: the nexus must exist between the government and the challenged activity. See, e.g., Blum v. Yaretsky, 457 U.S. 991, 1004 (1982); Rendell-Baker v. Kohn, 457 U.S. 830, 832 (1982). The defendant in Rendell-Baker was a heavily state-funded and regulated school; public funds accounted for between 90-99% of the school's operating budget. Id. at 832, 840-41. The State also had the power to approve some of the school's employment decisions. Id. But when a discharged employee sued the State for wrongful termination, this Court found insufficient government involvement to constitute state action by the defendant school. Id. at 841. The Court based its decision largely on the fact that the "decisions to discharge the petitioners were not compelled or even influenced by any state regulation." Id. at 841. The lack of a close nexus between the state and the challenged action – the termination of the employees – was dispositive. See id.

The government involvement in the particular action challenged is more central to a finding of close nexus than government regulation and financial support. Blum v. Yaretsky, 457 U.S. at 1004. In Blum, several nursing home patients sued a nursing home that had decided, pursuant to state regulations, to transfer the patients to a lower-cost facility. The state had licensed the home and had paid 90% of the patients' medical expenses, but this Court found insufficient ties to the government to find state action. Id. at 1005. Despite regulations that encouraged nursing homes to transfer eligible patients to lower-cost facilities, the Court noted that the "regulations themselves do not dictate the decision to discharge or transfer in a particular case." Id. at 1010. The Blum Court decided that the mere "fact of regulation" is insufficient to demonstrate that the government is "responsible for decisions made by the entity in the course of its business." Id. at 1011. Thus, state action can be found only when a close nexus exists between the state and the particular, challenged action of the regulated entity.

Amtrak cannot be found to be a state actor because almost no nexus, let alone a close nexus, exists between the federal government and Amtrak's decision to refuse to display Lebron's work. Mr. DeAngelo, the Amtrak employee who made the decision, is not a federal employee, nor is he on Amtrak's board of directors. Congress made it a goal of Amtrak's to use its <u>own</u> "best business judgment in taking actions to minimize Federal subsidies," 45 U.S.C. § 501a(1) (1988), but neither Congress nor Amtrak's board played any part in the challenged action: the decision to deny Lebron access to the Spectacular.

Like the defendants in <u>Rendell-Baker</u> and <u>Blum</u>, Amtrak was not subject to any particular government direction in reference to the challenged action. Mr. DeAngelo made the decision alone, without reference to any government guidelines. Unlike the defendant in <u>Burton</u>, Amtrak was not making a decision that was an "indispensable element in the financial success" of the federal government when it rejected Lebron's artwork. Amtrak's decision to reject the artwork resulted in no financial benefit of any kind to the federal government.

Thus, because there was neither a financial nor a regulatory "close nexus" between the federal government and Mr. DeAngelo's decision to reject Lebron's billboard art, there is not a "symbiotic relationship" between the government and Amtrak, and Amtrak is not a state actor.

A. **Officer Newsome violated Robinette's fourth amendment rights because his detention of Robinette lasted longer than was necessary to effectuate the purpose of the traffic stop.**

The nature of Newsome's detention of Robinette far exceeded the scope of the traffic stop. Newsome implicated the Fourth Amendment when he lawfully pulled Robinette over for speeding. *See Whren v. United States*, 116 S.Ct. 1769, 1772 (1996) ("temporary detention of individuals during the stop of an automobile . . . constitutes a 'seizure' of 'persons' within the meaning of [the Fourth Amendment]"). This Court has required that in order for the reasonableness requirement of the Fourth Amendment to be met, an investigative detention must be both temporary, which means that it "last no longer than is necessary to effectuate the purpose of the stop," and it must be limited in scope, which means that the investigative methods used must be the "lease intrusive means reasonably available." *Florida v. Royer*, 460 U.S. 491, 500 (1983); *see also Terry v. Ohio*, 392 U.S. 1, 19 (1968) (holding that the "scope of the search must be 'strictly tied to and justified by' the circumstances which rendered its initiation possible"). If either the length or the scope of the detention is not justified by the reasons supporting the detention in the first place, and if during the encounter the officer has formed no articulable suspicion that criminal activity is afoot, then the point at which the original detention should have been concluded marks the beginning of an unconstitutional detention. *See Royer*, 460 U.S. at 498-501.

When analyzing the constitutionality of the scope of a detention, courts have examined whether the officer has retained the citizen's important papers longer than necessary, and whether an officer who removes a detainee to a new location has a justifiable reason for the request to move.

Inspecting important papers, such as a driver's license and registration, is permissible, *see INS v. Delgado*, 466 U.S. 21, 216 (1984), but retaining them longer than necessary is not. *See Royer*, 460 U.S. at 503-04 (noting that the scope of the investigative detention was exceeded because the officers retained Royer's plane ticket and identification). "Longer than necessary" appears to center around whether the officer returned the important papers soon after the purpose for inspecting them in the first place was satisfied. Thus, in a 1991 case, this Court held that officers acted properly when they inspected the defendant's ticket and identification, and upon finding them to match and to be unremarkable, promptly returned them. *Florida v. Bostick*, 501 U.S. 429, 431

(1991). Similarly, the Tenth Circuit held that an officer acted in accordance with the fourth amendment when, during a traffic stop, the officer promptly returned the driver's license and registration after he found no problems with them. *United States v. Werking,* 915 F.2d 1404, 1408 (10th Cir. 1990). Conversely, in *Royer*, the officers failed to promptly return the defendant's ticket and driver's license, even though they appeared to be legitimate. 460 U.S. at 503-04.

Newsome retained Robinette's driver's license well beyond the point which justified his request for it. Newsome testified that "unless there was something wrong with his driver's license or something out of the ordinary," he intended to issue Robinette a warning. Record 18. Thus, after having found no problems with the driver's license, Newsome should have returned the driver's license upon approaching Robinette's car a second time. However, Newsome did not return the driver's license at that time; instead, he had Robinette step to the rear of his car, Record 11, and made him wait a number of minutes while Newsome returned to his cruiser to manually activate the video camera. Record 19. Robinette testified that the purpose of the video camera was to videotape requests to search for contraband. Record 19-20. It was not until Newsome returned from his cruise for a third time that he returned Robinette's driver's license. Record 11, 13. Thus, Officer Newsome kept Robinette's important papers -- his driver's license -- well beyond the time necessary.

Officer Newsome's behavior was unconstitutional not only because he failed to return Robinette's driver's license promptly, but because his reason for delaying the return of the driver's license had nothing to do with the justification for inspecting it in the first place. Newsome had legally detained Robinette for speeding, and in conjunction with a traffic stop, he had inspected Robinette's driver's license. The reason for delaying return of the license – having Robinette step to the rear of his vehicle and wait a number of minutes – was to videotape a request to search. As in *Royer*, the relationship between the request for important papers and the reason for delaying their return is far too tenuous to allow the latter to piggyback upon the legal authority of the former.

Officer Newsome's detention of Robinette also went beyond the scope of a constitutionally permissible detention because Officer Newsome had no justifiable reason for his request that Robinette leave his car and stand between his car and the police cruiser. An officer may exercise his or her legal authority over a citizen by removing the citizen from the location in which he or she was when first approached, for example, by asking that a citizen leave his or her car, *see Pennsylvania v. Mimms*, 434 U.S. 106 (1977), or by conducting a pat down search for weapons, *see Terry v. Ohio*, 392 U.S. 1, 27 (1968). However, the officer may exercise this authority only to extent that doing so ensures the officer's safety while conducting the investigative detention. *See Mimms*, 434 U.S. at 110; *Terry*, 392 U.S. at 27.

The facts surrounding the *Mimms* encounter emphasize the fact that Newsome's request that Robinette stand to the rear of his car was entirely unrelated to the detention for speeding. In *Mimms*, the officer as a matter of habit requested that persons exit the car *at the inception* of the investigative detention. *Mimms*, 434 U.S. at 109-10. The Court characterized making a person wait outside of his or her car rather than siting inside as a *de minimis* intrusion, justified by the "inordinate risk confronting an officer as he approaches a person seated in an automobile." *Id.* at 110. Because the intrusion was minimal, and because it was justified by a legitimate reason, the *Mimms* court found that the requirement that searches and seizures be reasonable was met for Fourth Amendment purposes. *Id.* at 111. Officer Newsome's request that Robinette leave his car was not justified by any "inordinate risk."

Unlike Mimms, who was asked to leave his car at the beginning of the traffic stop, Robinette was not asked to exit his vehicle until after Newsome had obtained his driver's license and had run a check on it. Newsome testified that he had planned to give Robinette a warning when he pulled Robinette over, absent a problem with his license check. Record 18. The subjective intent of an officer does not calculate into Fourth Amendment analysis. *See Whren v. United States*, 116 S.Ct. 1769, 1774 (1996). However, the fact that Newsome asked Robinette to exit his car after running the check on his license, finding no problems, and determining to give Robinette a warning rather than a citation, means that Newsome extended the initial detention for reasons entirely removed from safety. Newsome's behavior when he elected to allow Robinette to remain in his car while he verified that Robinette's license had no problems strongly indicates that he had no fears for his safety. When Officer Newsome asked Robinette to exit the car, all that remained to complete the detention justified by Robinette's speeding was to return Robinette's driver's license and issue a warning. Precisely because issuing a warning rather than a citation functions to "cut [the detainee] some slack," Transcript at 1, Newsome would have had no reasonable basis to fear for his safety at the time he asked Robinette to leave his car. In fact, nothing in Officer Newsome's testimony indicates that he feared for his safety.

In addition to the fact that he did not fear his safety, Newsome's request that Robinette exit his car was constitutionally obnoxious because the reason for using his authority over Robinette had nothing at all to do with the traffic stop. The *Royer* Court held that the removal of the defendant from the concourse to the small room would have been acceptable if it had been done for "reasons of safety and security," *Royer*, 460 U.S. at 505, but instead, Royer's relocation was used as an *"attempt to gain his consent to search his luggage." Id.* at 505 (emphasis added). Similarly, the *sole purpose* for asking Robinette to exit his car and wait between it and the cruiser while Newsome activated the video camera was to record his request for consent to search for drugs. Record 19-20.

Newsome's conduct during his interaction with Robinette violates the fundamental principle of the Fourth Amendment -- that searches or seizures be limited, in length and scope, to the reasons justifying the use of legal authority in the first place. Newsome had the authority to pull Robinette over for speeding, and Newsome had the authority to inspect Robinette's driver's license. Newsome did not have the authority to remove Robinette from his vehicle. He did not need to do so in order to complete the investigative effort he undertook -- he just as easily could have returned Robinette's driver's license through the car window. He had not developed any articulable suspicion that Robinette was transporting contraband, nor did he fear that Robinette was a threat to his safety, either of which might have justified removing Robinette from his vehicle. Rather, Newsome removed Robinette from his vehicle for a reason entirely unrelated to the traffic violation of speeding, and by doing so, violated Robinette's Fourth Amendment rights. Therefore, Officer Newsome illegally detained Robinette.

2.   Officer Newsome violated Robinette's fourth amendment rights because his encounter with Robinette violated this Court's length and justification requirements.

The nature of Newsome's detention of Robinette far exceeded the scope of the traffic stop. Newsome implicated the Fourth Amendment when he lawfully pulled Robinette over for speeding. *See Whren v. United States*, 116 S.Ct. 1769, 1772 (1996) ("temporary detention of individuals during the stop of an automobile . . . constitutes a 'seizure' of 'persons' within the meaning of [the Fourth Amendment]"). This Court has required that in order for the reasonableness requirement of the Fourth Amendment to be met, an investigative detention must be both temporary, which means that it "last no longer than is necessary to effectuate the purpose of the stop," and it must be limited in scope, which means that the investigative methods used must be the "lease intrusive means reasonably available." *Florida v. Royer*, 460 U.S. 491, 500 (1983); *see also Terry v. Ohio*, 392 U.S. 1, 19 (1968) (holding that the "scope of the search must be 'strictly tied to and justified by' the circum-stances which rendered its initiation possible"). If either the length or the scope of the detention is not justified by the reasons supporting the detention in the first place, and if during the encounter the officer has formed no articulable suspicion that criminal activity is afoot, then the point at which the original detention should have been concluded marks the beginning of an unconstitutional detention. *See Royer*, 460 U.S. at 498-501.

When analyzing the constitutionality of the scope of a detention, courts have examined whether the officer has retained the citizen's important papers longer than necessary, and whether an officer who removes a detainee to a new location has safety or security reasons that justify the request to move. [cite] Officer Newsome violated both of these standards.

a. Officer Newsome retained Robinette's papers longer than necessary.

Inspecting important papers, such as a driver's license and registration, is permissible, *see INS v. Delgado*, 466 U.S. 21, 216 (1984), but retaining them longer than necessary is not. *See Royer*, 460 U.S. at 503-04 (noting that the scope of the investigative detention was exceeded because the officers retained Royer's plane ticket and identification). "Longer than necessary" appears to center around whether the officer returned the important papers soon after the purpose for inspecting them in the first place was satisfied. Thus, in a 1991 case, this Court held that officers acted properly when they inspected the defendant's ticket and identification, and upon finding them to match and to be unremarkable, promptly returned them. *Florida v. Bostick*, 501 U.S. 429, 431 (1991). Similarly, the Tenth Circuit held that an officer acted in accordance with the fourth amendment when, during a traffic stop, the officer promptly returned the driver's license and registration after he found no problems with them. *United States v. Werking*, 915 F.2d 1404, 1408 (10th Cir. 1990). Conversely, in *Royer*, the officers violated a suspect's rights when they failed to promptly return the defendant's ticket and driver's license, even though they appeared to be legitimate. 460 U.S. at 503-04.

Newsome retained Robinette's driver's license much longer than necessary. Newsome testified that "unless there was something wrong with his driver's license or something out of the ordinary," he intended to issue Robinette a warning. Record 18. Thus, after having found no problems with the driver's license, Newsome should have returned the driver's license upon approaching Robinette's car a second time. However, Newsome did not return the driver's license at that time; instead, he had Robinette step to the rear of his car, Record 11, and made him wait a number of minutes while Newsome returned to his cruiser to manually activate the video camera. Record 19. Robinette testified that the purpose of the video camera was to videotape requests to search for contraband. Record 19-20. It was not until Newsome returned from his cruise for a third time that he returned Robinette's driver's license. Record 11, 13. Thus, Officer Newsome kept Robinette's important papers – his driver's license – well beyond the time necessary.

> **b.** **Officer Newsome had no safety or security reasons to justify his request that Robinette leave his car.**

Officer Newsome's detention of Robinette also went beyond the scope of a constitutionally permissible detention because Officer Newsome had no safety or security reason that justified his request that Robinette leave his car and stand between his car and the police cruiser. An officer may exercise his or her legal authority over a citizen by removing the citizen from the location in which he or she was when first approached, for example, by asking that a citizen leave his or her car, *see Pennsylvania v. Mimms*, 434 U.S. 106 (1977), or by conducting a pat down search for weapons, *see Terry v. Ohio*, 392 U.S. 1, 27 (1968). However, the officer may exercise this authority only to the extent that doing so ensures the officer's safety while conducting the investigative detention. *See Mimms*, 434 U.S. at 110; *Terry*, 392 U.S. at 27.

The *Mimms* decision makes clear that safety and security reasons alone can justify an officer's request to move a person to a new location. In *Mimms*, the officer as a matter of habit requested that persons exit the car *at the inception* of the investigative detention. *Mimms*, 434 U.S. at 109-10. The Court characterized making a person wait outside of his or her car rather than siting inside as a *de minimis* intrusion, justified by the "inordinate risk confronting an officer as he approaches a person seated in an automobile." *Id.* at 110. Because the intrusion was minimal, and because it was justified by safety reasons, the *Mimms* court found that the requirement that searches and seizures be reasonable was met for Fourth Amendment purposes. *Id.* at 111.

Following similar reasoning, the *Royer* Court held that the removal of the defendant from the concourse to the small room would have been acceptable if it had been done for "reasons of safety and security." *Royer*, 460 U.S. at 505. Instead, the Court noted, Royer's relocation was used as an "*attempt to gain his consent to search his luggage.*" *Id.* (emphasis added). Because the removal was not justified by reasons of safety or security, the court found it unconstitutional. *Id.*

Officer Newsome's request that Robinette leave his car was not justified by any "inordinate risk," or by any safety or security reasons. Unlike Mimms, who was asked to leave his car at the beginning of the traffic stop, Robinette was not asked to exit his vehicle until after Newsome had obtained his driver's license and had run a check on it. Newsome testified that he had planned to give Robinette a warning when he pulled Robinette over, absent a problem with his license check. Record 18. The subjective intent of an officer does not calculate into Fourth Amendment analysis. *See Whren v. United States*, 116 S. Ct. 1769, 1774 (1996) (parenthetical description). However, the fact that Newsome asked Robinette to exit his car after running the check on his license, finding no problems, and determining to give Robinette a warning rather than a citation, means that Newsome extended the initial detention for reasons entirely removed from safety.

Newsome's behavior when he elected to allow Robinette to remain in his car while he verified that Robinette's license had no problems strongly indicates that he had no fears for his safety. When Officer Newsome asked Robinette to exit the car, all that remained to complete the detention justified by Robinette's speeding was to return Robinette's driver's license and issue a warning. Precisely because issuing a warning rather than a citation functions to "cut [the detainee] some slack," Transcript at 1, Newsome would have had no reasonable basis to fear for his safety at the time he asked Robinette to leave his car. In fact, nothing in Officer Newsome's testimony indicates that he feared for his safety.

In addition to the fact that he did not fear his safety, Newsome's request that Robinette exit his car was constitutionally obnoxious because the reason for using his authority over Robinette had nothing at all to do with the traffic stop. Like the purpose of the request in *Royer*, Newsome's *sole purpose* for asking Robinette to exit his car and wait between it and the cruiser while Newsome activated the video camera was to record his request for consent to search for drugs. Record 19-20. No safety or security reasons justified the request.

Newsome's conduct during his interaction with Robinette violated the fundamental principle of the Fourth Amendment -- that searches or seizures be limited, in length and scope, to the reasons justifying the use of legal authority in the first place. Newsome had the authority to pull Robinette over for speeding, and Newsome had the authority to inspect Robinette's driver's license. Newsome did not have the authority to remove Robinette from his vehicle. He did not need to do so in order to complete the investigative effort he undertook -- he just as easily could have returned Robinette's driver's license through the car window. He had not developed any articulable suspicion that Robinette was transporting contraband, nor did he fear that Robinette was a threat to his safety, either of which might have justified removing Robinette from his vehicle. Rather, Newsome removed Robinette from his vehicle for a reason entirely unrelated to the traffic violation of speeding, and by doing so, violated Robinette's Fourth Amendment rights. Therefore, Officer Newsome illegally detained Robinette.

Chapter Eight
Following Format Rules

Possible Teaser for Syllabus:

It's hard to come up with a teaser for this chapter. I often combine it with the self-grading chapter because I deal with it quickly. You might ask students to "be able to explain the use of the term *passim*" (Section 8.4.5 or Section 8.5.5); in the alternative, you might ask students which Supreme Court rule governs some particular aspect of the brief, e.g., the cover (rule 34.1) or the Certificate of Service (rule 29.5).

Learning Goals of Class Meeting:

Make students aware of the importance of format rules, both formal and informal, national and local.
Identify significant format rules, and the requirements which are most often not met (by attorneys or students).

Changes from Second Edition:

In this edition, the formal requirements for appellate briefs and formal requirements for motion briefs are presented in two separate sections. Although this change has resulted in some repetition, the change allows teachers to assign students to read either Section 8.4 *or* Section 8.5 to learn relevant formal requirements. The text brings in more examples of local rules and discusses courtesy copies and electronic filing in a bit more detail.

Audio-visual aids on the website: N/A

Ideas for Class Discussion/Visual Aids:

I do not spend a great deal of time with this chapter; providing a sample brief answers most questions. Putting relevant pages from a brief on a document camera can help address more difficult format issues. To involve the class, ask questions designed to point out common problems or misunderstandings, e.g., "Why does it say writ of certiorari "to" and not "from" the lower court?" "When is *passim* appropriate?" "What do you do if one of the opinions below is not yet reported?" etc.

Identify which format requirements will be unfamiliar to your students, e.g., tables of contents and authorities. Because judges and law clerks depend on formal requirements to help them use the briefs, it is vital that formal requirements are met and that tables are accurate and readable, If your students have never completed certificates of service, you might want to spend a moment reassuring them of their simplicity (looking at a sample goes a long way toward solving that problem). You may have particular course service requirements. In my course, service is not valid without all the needed copies, and thus students learn that they must finish their briefs in time to have copies made (not a major problem, with 24-hour copy shops). This requirement is realistic, as many courts do not accept service until all needed copies are filed.

In these days of electronic filing, you might want to spend some time on why and how courts ask for attorneys' signatures, in particular if you will be penalizing students for failing to sign the document properly, whether electronically or in ink. If you want to spend more time on format requirements, you could review an article cited in the text: Judith D. Fischer, *Bareheaded and Barefaced Counsel: Courts React to Unprofessionalism in Lawyers' Papers*, 31 Suffolk Univ. L. Rev. 1 (1997). This article identifies many common attorney failures, both format and substantive.

During the past couple of years, I have required students to serve a copy of their final draft on their opponent. They set up the exchange via e-mail, copying their teacher. Many students have fun with the exchange, using overly formal language ("My Dear Ms. Opponent") or making up interesting reasons for the time they wish to schedule ("because I have a deposition in Paris on Wednesday afternoon. . . . ."). The requirement gives me the opportunity to discuss many relevant professionalism issues.

There are a couple of obvious problems that can arise from this method and that I try to avoid. First, there is the concern that a student will use another student's work inappropriately. We require that students exchange hard copies rather than digital copies for this reason. We also counsel them that they are to use the opponent's draft only for oral argument preparation and that they are not to give it or show it to anyone else. Second, students are worried that their opponents will ridicule their writing. We discuss this directly in class as we discuss professionalism. This discussion cannot prevent all unprofessional behavior, but I believe it is an enlightening discussion for many students.

Third, there is the problem of students who are having personal or academic difficulties and who do not have a brief to exchange for this reason. Because these are situations that may occur in real life – they may sometimes have to cancel an appointment or file a motion for an extension – I require most students in this situation to keep their opponent informed in some limited way. I do not require that they reveal personal information, but I have them send their opponent a note saying, e.g., "my paper will be available for exchange on date," OR "I have received permission to withdraw from Appellate Advocacy. Professor Beazley will contact you about a new oral argument opponent." In class, we have discussed generally the many non-gossip-worthy reasons that people have late papers or withdraw, and I also counsel students that they are not to talk to others about personal information that they may learn about an opponent. The reality is that these situations occur – and are talked about – whether or not students exchange papers. Of course, if a student has a true emergency or a particularly difficult situation, I relieve the student of the duty of corresponding with his or her opponent.

New vocabulary words:
> *passim*
> Certificate of Service
> Certificate of Compliance

Chapter Nine
Special Teams: Questions Presented, Statement of the Case, Summary of the Argument, Point Headings

Possible Teaser(s) for Syllabus:

What makes Judge Hamilton's blood boil? (Section 9.2.1)

In what section of the brief should you use the buddy system, and how does it work? (Section 9.2.3(b))

Why was it mean to record that the Captain was sober? (Section 9.2.3)

How is Pointillism relevant to legal writing? (Section 9.2.3(b))

Teaching Goals:

Communicate unique writing requirements for special elements in the brief.

Introduce persuasive writing techniques that can be used appropriately in certain elements of the brief.

Changes from Second Edition:

This chapter now illustrates how to incorporate language from a pleading standard for a motion into a question presented. In the section on the statement of facts, the chapter introduces concepts of narrative reasoning and storytelling theory, citing some of the relevant scholarship on this matter.

Pre-class assignment other than the readings:

I usually ask the class to e-mail me a question presented for their case in which they (a) use at least one persuasive method discussed in the chapter and (b) explain their use of the persuasive method. Unless instructed otherwise, many students will claim their use of "under-does-when" or "whether" as their persuasive method. While this choice can be made for a persuasive reason, you might want to encourage (or require) that they use and explain a persuasive method beyond this basic decision. In addition or in the alternative, you can require them to complete a fact statement, a summary of the argument, or parts of them, asking the students to label their persuasive techniques.

Audio-visual aids on the website:

The website contains a powerpoint that you can use to lead a discussion on questions presented (but not introductory statements). The powerpoint will have some blank pages on which you can insert class examples to use for discussion.

Ideas for Class Discussion:

This chapter covers a lot of information. You may wish to spend more than one class session addressing the chapter, particularly if you have enough time to allow group work on any of the elements discussed. This chapter might be a good time to discuss the dangers of going overboard in persuasive techniques. You may also want to have students **e-mail you examples of their own writing the day before your class meeting** so that you can use their writing as fodder for class discussion. Specific ideas are addressed below.

1. Motion Brief Introductions:

The powerpoint addresses questions presented only. It does not contain sample bad motion brief introductions; these are much easier to write than questions presented. If you collect student samples, you may want to address issues of length (how much detail is appropriate in an introduction?), specificity (can the reader tell what issues are relevant to the motion as opposed to the merits?), and persuasiveness (how much "argument" is appropriate in the introduction?).

2. Questions Presented:

The three problems illustrated in the text are particularly common when students try to write persuasive questions presented: 1) they assume elements at issue; 2) they go too far in their persuasiveness; and 3) they write over-long questions. I almost think that these mistakes are a necessary part of the learning process, so I try very hard to take the time to allow the students to take a crack at writing their own questions. I encourage them to stretch their persuasiveness to the limit, because there will be no consequences if they go too far for a class exercise. Before I show their attempts, I soften them up by showing them my edited examples of student questions from the Minnesota v. Carter case. For each question, I ask them how they can tell which side wrote the question, and whether the writer wants an answer of "yes," "no," or "heavens, of course not!" As we discuss the effectiveness of the questions, we also look for enthymemes, use of concrete facts, positions of emphasis, and other persuasive writing techniques.

These questions provide a lot of laughs, because going too far in persuasiveness often creates unintentional humor. I tell them that for the exercise I *hope* someone will go too far, because going too far teaches everyone something about the limits of persuasion, and it's a good lesson. If I have a two-hour session, I may discuss the examples and then have the students create their questions in an in-class exercise, perhaps as group work. Otherwise, I might have them send me their questions via e-mail before the meeting and show them my samples before looking at class samples. However I collect the questions, I post representative examples of good and "bad" questions, and we discuss them in the same way that we have discussed the Minnesota v. Carter questions. I find that seeing the humor in the Minnesota v. Carter questions makes the students more comfortable with good-natured criticism of their own efforts, and of course I follow my typical guidelines of anonymity and using only classic mistakes. As I noted in introductory material, if an example is greeted with instant laughter, I take pains to spread the blame, noting, for example, "yep, I got a bunch of questions that sounded like this!"

The examples below will be listed in order, with a set of petitioner questions followed by a set of respondent questions. Some or all of these questions are on the website powerpoint. You may want to download materials from the website and mix up the questions, testing the students' ability to evaluate which side wrote which question. On the other hand, because the answer to the "which side" question is often obvious, you may wish to do them in order, and begin your discussion of each question by saying, e.g., "okay, how do we know that this is a petitioner question? What are the clues?"

Examples of Attempts at Persuasive Petitioner Questions from Minnesota v. Carter, and possible points for discussion:

Should the Court reverse the court below, where defendants failed to demonstrate a "legitimate expectation of privacy," and when defendants' only purpose for being present in the apartment was to conduct an illicit drug transaction?

This is a petitioner question. In addition to various imperfections in writing, this question assumes an element at issue (that defendants "failed" to demonstrate a legitimate expectation of privacy). It is accurate, however, that the defendants' only purpose for being present was to bag drugs, which constitutes an illicit drug transaction. The writer properly placed this fact in a position of emphasis at the end of the question.

Under the fourth amendment, does a police officer's naked-eye observation of criminal activity inside a residence constitute a search if the officer viewed the activity from a public area outside the curtilage of the residence without the aid of any unreasonable measures?

This question is a classic "assumption of the issue" question. It essentially asks, "does a person violate a law if he does <u>not</u> do the things that violate the law? The writer presumes that the officer was outside the curtilage and that he did not use any "unreasonable" measures. This is the time to emphasize that a good question will provide the facts that the writer will use to establish that the standard has been met or not been met. The format should be "Whether result occurs under phrase-that-pays standard when these facts exist" rather than, "Whether result occurs when phrase-that-pays exists."

If the students are familiar enough with the facts of <u>Minnesota v. Carter</u>, you can ask them what facts should be used. For example, the "naked-eye observation" helps to establish that the officer used no unreasonable measures. The fact that he stood one and a half feet from the window in a common area may help establish that he was outside of the curtilage.

Under the Fourth Amendment, does a transient invitee into an apartment have a legitimate expectation of privacy within that residence when the only purpose for the occupancy is to conduct an illegal business transaction?

This question is well-written. A couple of enthymemes are suggested by the word choice – a "transient invitee" has less of an expectation of privacy than a "short-term guest," for example. The writer does not assume any elements at issue. Students might presume the "only reason" language is a problem, but the case's findings of fact established that the only reason for the visit was to bag the cocaine.

Should a police officer who can use his natural senses outside the curtilage of a residence to view illegal drug activity be asked that he not watch the activity because it constitutes a search?

This question comes close to acceptable – the use of "natural senses" creates a presumption of validity that helps the petitioners. However, the writer has assumed that the officer stood outside the curtilage. Substituting the actual location (e.g., in a common area, a foot and a half from the window) would solve this problem. The language about "be asked that he not watch" is a good "of course not!" question.

> Whether this court should enlarge the class of individuals who may claim exclusion of evidence under the Fourth Amendment to include short-term guests who are present on property only for the purpose of engaging in criminal activity.

This writer's use of the language "enlarge the class of individuals" preys on a presumption that most readers will think this is a bad idea. This writer used more everyday language than the writer of the "transient invitee" question above. Note that the "good facts" for the petitioner are in a position of emphasis.

> Are the illegal narcotics trafficking activities of two temporary, out-of-state visitors, which were conducted in the middle of a well-lit room with a window facing a common area, and which were observed by a police officer who stood outside the apartment in a common area and looked through the blinds of the window, shielded by the fourth amendment, which protects against only *unreasonable* searches and seizures?

This question is long, and it could be better-structured, but it does not assume elements at issue, and it emphasizes facts that are bad for the respondents and good for the petitioners – they were in the middle of a well-lit room, observable from a common area through blinds. You might ask students why the writer ended the question the way he or she did. Was the use of italics meant to provoke the reader to say "of course not! This search was perfectly reasonable given these facts." Could another structure been more effective?

Examples of Attempts at Persuasive Respondent Questions from Minnesota v. Carter, and possible points for discussion:

> Whether persons who are gathered together in a private home with the permission of the leaseholder to work together on a common task have a reasonable expectation of privacy sufficient to challenge a search by a government agent.

*I admit it; this is the most fun question. It provides the best object lesson in not going too far. And to top it off, it's based on language from the lower court opinion, showing that courts are not perfect, either. The students invariably laugh at this question, because it raises images that completely contradict the realities of the case. I will often sing a parody of a hymn, "we gather together to bag the cocai-aine." or point out that the words "work together on a common task" give the impression of a quilting bee or a barn-raising. This question provides good fodder for a discussion of questions that are technically accurate – as this one is – but still wrong. If a writer gives
the court an inaccurate impression through a cleverly worded question, his or her credibility will suffer when the Court discovers what the case is <u>really</u> about.*

> Whether citizens have a constitutionally protected right to be free from a police officer's unauthorized covert observation into a private dwelling when that citizen

reasonably expected and took measures to ensure that his activities would be shielded from the public's view.

This question uses words that conjure up very specific images – e.g., we certainly think of "citizens" as people who have more rights. Similarly, the words "private dwelling" create a different image than the words "basement apartment." You might engage students in a discussion of which other parts of the question do or don't cross the line. For example, the words "reasonably expected" probably assume an issue. On the other hand, because the search was without a warrant, is it accurate to say it was "unauthorized"?

Are Fourth Amendment privacy rights violated when an officer of the state peers through the blinds into a private home in order to clandestinely conduct surveillance on a host and her houseguests?

This question does not assume elements at issue. You might ask students whether the use of loaded words goes too far: "officer of the state," "peers [another word from the court below] through the blinds," "clandestinely conduct surveillance."

Does it constitute a search under the Fourth Amendment for a police officer to enter an area of the curtilage of a residence not normally used by the public, and place himself in a contorted position immediately outside the window of the residence, in order to view the activities within the residence through small gaps in an otherwise completely covered window of the residence?

This question assumes the element of "curtilage," but I don't believe it assumes other issues. Again, you might ask students whether it violates the "oh, come on!" standard (i.e., it goes too far) with the use of the words "place himself in a contorted position." On the other hand, the use of the accurate words "small gaps in an otherwise completely covered window" may lead the reader to presume that the residents took reasonable steps to maintain their privacy.

Does a person who is invited into the home of another have a right to be secure in that home from unreasonable searches and seizures, as provided in the Fourth Amendment to the United States Constitution?

This question probably illustrates the basic question the Court wanted to answer with this case: "Does being a guest create an expectation of privacy in someone else's home?" You might ask the students whether the writer could have used phrasing or details to make the question more persuasive, or whether the bad facts for the respondent make this a situation for "least said, soonest mended."

Does the Fourth Amendment's prohibition of unreasonable searches and seizures apply to a police officer, who without a search warrant, walks off of a pathway, across a lawn, and then wedges himself between a bush and a building, in order to peek into a home from a distance of 12-18 inches?

This question is technically accurate, and I think reasonable minds can differ over whether it goes too far. All of the details are accurate, but the words "wedge" and "peek" might be too over-dramatic. You might ask students what they would substitute (e.g., "place" and "look").

3. Statement of the Case:

The issues that you highlight when discussing the statement of the case may vary depending on the case that the students are working on. If their fact statement is particularly complicated, you might discuss organization, perhaps having them identify possible topics for a topical organization. You might also have them list good facts and bad facts for their client's argument. If there are particularly significant "good facts" or "bad facts" for one side or another, you might have them break into petitioner/respondent groups and try using persuasive techniques to write them up.

If you wish to discuss storytelling theory with your students, you might try to identify possible schemas that exist in the client's situation, possible goals that one side or the other could have (and ways that the opposite side is trying to thwart that goal) and telling details that either side might like to highlight.

If this is impractical, you may ask them to write up some respondent facts from <u>Miller v. Albright</u>. For example, a tough "bad fact" for the petitioners is that the plaintiff's father had not followed the necessary rules to establish his paternity until it was too late under government rules. A student-petitioner relays these facts as follows (See Appendix C in text):

Petitioner Lorelyn Penero Miller was born on June 20, 1970, in the Republic of the Phillippines. App. 15. Her mother, Luz Penero, was a citizen of the Republic of the Phillippines. <u>Id.</u> Her father, Charlie R. Miller, is a citizen of the United States and was so at the time of Ms. Miller's birth. Mr. Miller and Ms. Miller's mother were never married; Ms. Miller's birth certificate does not list the name or nationality of her father as a result. App. 15. On July 27, 1992, Mr. Miller obtained a voluntary paternity decree from a court in his home state of Texas establishing that Ms. Miller is his daughter.

In 1986, 8 U.S.C. § 1409(a)(4) was amended to lower from twenty-one to eighteen the age limit that restricted a father's ability to pass his citizenship to a foreign-born child. Because of the effective date of that amendment, Ms. Miller would be able to satisfy 8 U.S.C. § 1409(a)(4) if she met its requirements before she turned twenty-one.

On February 11, 1992, Ms. Miller applied to the United States Department of State for registration as a United States citizen and for the issuance of a passport. App. 16. The State Department ultimately denied her application on November 5, 1992, because (1) Ms. Miller had failed to obtain the paternity decree before Ms. Miller's twenty-first birthday as required by 8 U.S.C. § 1409(a)(4), and (2) Mr. Miller had failed to agree in writing (while Ms. Miller was still under twenty-one) that he would financially support her until she turned twenty-one. App. 8. Mr. Miller was denied the opportunity to pass his United States citizenship to his daughter simply because he was late completing some paperwork and because he is a man. The paperwork obstacles that Mr. Miller failed to negotiate apply only to fathers; if Mr.

Miller were a mother, Ms. Miller would have been a citizen from birth.

Ask the students to write up approximately this same set of facts from the respondent's point of view. They must take care to be accurate and not to go too far. Here is one possible answer:

> Petitioner Lorelyn Penero Miller was born on June 20, 1970, in the Republic of the Phillippines. App. 15. Her mother was Luz Penero, a citizen of the Republic of the Phillippines. Id. No father's name was recorded on her birth certificate. Id. The record does not indicate any contact between Ms. Miller and her alleged father until almost twenty-two years had passed. On February 11, 1992, when Ms. Miller had reached the age of twenty-one years and eight months, she applied to the United States Department of State for registration as a United States citizen and for the issuance of a passport. App. 16. She apparently based this request on the provisions of 8 U.S.C. § 1409 that allow children of U.S. citizen fathers to claim citizenship if they meet certain standards before they reach twenty-one years of age. On July 27, 1992, more than a month after Ms. Miller's twenty-second birthday, Mr. Miller obtained a voluntary paternity decree from a court in his home state of Texas establishing that Ms. Miller is his daughter. App. 17. Interestingly, the record does not indicate any contact between Ms. Miller and Mr. Miller until after she had applied for citizenship. Id. The Court denied her request on November 5 of that year. Id.

In the alternative, if you don't want the students to take the time to write up an example from Miller v. Albright, you could contrast these two examples and ask them to analyze whether either one goes too far. For example, the writer of the second example may have wanted the reader to conclude that Mr. Miller and Ms. Miller do not have a genuine father-daughter relationship, and that she is only using him to establish U.S. citizenship. Does the observation achieve this goal when it points out that Mr. Miller did not officially establish his paternity until after his daughter had applied for citizenship? Does the writer go too far in the way he or she makes the observation? "Illegitimacy," as courts described it then, is a sensitive issue (obviously, because you may have some students in your class whose parents were unmarried at the time of their birth, you will want to be delicate in how you discuss this issue), so you might want to discuss how far a writer can go without crossing the line.

When discussing using persuasive writing techniques in their own fact statements, you might ask two questions. First, what legal conclusions does each side need the reader to draw? Second, what facts might lead the reader to draw those conclusions? For example, in Minnesota v. Carter, the petitioner wants the reader to believe that the Office was not inside the home's curtilage when he looked through the window. Thus, she must use the facts about his location and how he got to that location to try to make the reader draw the conclusion that it was not a location "associated with the intimacies of the home." Notice how the petitioner describes the situation in her statement of the case:

> On May 15, 1994, a confidential informant reported to Officer Jim Thielen that drug activity was occurring in a nearby apartment. See Record E-1. The informant specified that he or she had viewed the occupants of 3943 South Valley View, Apartment 103, sitting at a table placing a white powdery substance into

plastic bags. See Record E-2. The informant, who also gave the officer details about a car the informant believed the apartment occupants were using, said that he or she had seen the drug activity from outside the apartment's ground-level window when the informant had walked past the window. Record G-9, G-39.

At approximately 8:00 p.m., in response to the informant's report, the officer drove to the apartment complex and then walked on a grassy common area to a spot one to one and a half feet from the window of Apartment 103. Record G-45, G-13. From his location in the apartment complex yard, Officer Thielen could see into the interior of Apartment 103. Record E-2. At no time during his observation did Officer Thielen place his hands along the window. Record G-13. He used no flashlight or other device to supplement his natural senses. Id.

Though the grassy area on which Officer Thielen stood featured some shrubs and trees, the shrubs were not planted immediately in front of the apartment window to create an enclosure that prevented the public from gaining entrance to the area. See Record E-10. The area outside the window was one on which residents and non-residents regularly walked and interacted with others. Record G-44, G-32, G-68. Children commonly played there, and on at least one occasion a bicycle was left directly outside Thompson's window. Record G-71.

Ask the students to identify factual details that would lead a reader to conclude that the place Officer Thielen stood was outside the home's curtilage. Notice how the respondent describes the same scene:

On May 15, 1994, Officer Jim Thielen of the Eagan, Minnesota Police Department received information from an unidentified source that the source had observed people inside a nearby apartment "bagging" a white powdery substance. Record E-2. The source also stated that a blue Cadillac parked at the apartment building belonged to the individuals inside the apartment. Record E-2. After collecting additional information from the source, Officer Thielen proceeded to the apartment in question. The officer was able to approach a window belonging to the apartment by leaving the sidewalk leading up to the building, walking onto the grass and behind bushes located two to four feet away from the window. Record G-43.

By standing approximately twelve to eighteen inches from the window, Officer Thielen was able to observe the occupants' activities inside the apartment for approximately fifteen minutes. Record E-2, G-53. He then returned to his original location at a nearby fire station parking lot, where he contacted a superior officer to inform him of his findings and to request instructions. Record G-53, G-54.

What details does the respondent include, or what words does the respondent use, to encourage the reader to draw the conclusion that the Officer was inside the curtilage when he looked through the window? Did either writer go too far? Could either writer have done more?

If your students are writing motion briefs, you may want to spend some time noting how much detail to go into, and how to address facts which are more relevant to the merits, vs. facts that are more relevant to the motion. In addition, as the text notes, you may want to address the difficulty of talking about facts that must be taken as true for the purposes of the motion, even though there have been no findings as to these facts. It might be fruitful to take a particular fact or set of facts and have each side write them up, either before or during class.

4. Summary of the Argument

The main problem that most students have with the summary of the argument is keeping it short. They start to explain their arguments, and the next thing they know, it's five pages later. The summaries in Appendix C are all rather short, but you might go to an on-line resource and find a Supreme Court brief with a long summary. Ask the students to condense it. In the alternative, ask students to spend twenty minutes writing a summary of their own argument. The best way to do this is probably to ask them to write it without consulting their briefs – They should concentrate only on the most significant points. Perhaps you could ask them to use their point headings only as a basis for the summary (pointing out, of course, that the rules specifically state that the summary should *not* just restate the point headings).

The second problem students have when writing the summary is adopting an argumentative tone. A good, short in-class exercise would be to break the students into petitioner and respondent groups and ask them to write a dramatic opening sentence for the summary of the argument. You could have the groups write their sentences on the board or place them on an overhead projector to share with the class. I encourage the students to "push the envelope" a little bit when writing these sentences. The results are often very revealing of the presumptions that the writer's client brings to the case. It might be interesting to have the students complete this assignment *before* you talk about the fact statement. Having in mind the presumptions that each side brings to the case might be instructive as students contemplate what story they need to tell with the fact statement.

In the alternative, ask students to look at the last sample appellate brief and have them write an introductory sentence to the *opponent's* summary of the argument. For example, the Miller v. Albright petitioner opens his summary of the argument by stating:

Congress may not use an irrebuttable gender stereotype to implement its policy decisions, even if those policy decisions concern immigration law.

The respondent might open the summary by stating:

This Court should not overrule a longstanding decision of this Court that respects the authority of Congress to legislate matters of immigration.

In another case, Knowles v. Iowa, the Court reviewed an Iowa statute allowing police to conduct searches of automobiles whenever an arrest was possible (e.g., for a speeding ticket). A writer representing Iowa could begin the summary by writing a paragraph that makes his position clear:

This Court should permit an arrest-level search in situations in which an arrest is allowed, but not made. When an officer has the authority to arrest – and the authority to conduct a full search incident to that arrest – the officer should also have the authority to search when issuing a citation in lieu of that arrest.

The petitioner might have started the argument by focusing on the trivial types of arrests that would allow a search:

> Police officers should not have blanket authority to conduct a search incident to a traffic ticket.

As was discussed in the section on questions presented above, sometimes students learn more about persuasion when they go too far. If some of your students write outrageous sentences in response to this exercise, praise them for taking chances before addressing the ways in which they need to tone things down.

5. Point Headings:

The two main problems students have with point headings is a) failure to make them case-specific and b) failure to keep them short. Once again, you may want to look for briefs on-line and ask students to write better point headings than the ones included in the briefs. In the alternative, you might ask them to revise this set of point headings from the respondent's brief in Minnesota v. Carter:

II.   A police officer conducts a search within the meaning of the Fourth Amendment when he observes actions taking place inside a private residence from within inches of the residence's window, because the area is so close to the home that it qualifies as part of the residence's curtilage.

    A.   The observations of Respondents' activities constitute an unwarranted search because the police officer invaded the curtilage of the apartment by being physically within inches of the apartment's window and walls, having left the normal walkway area to do so.

    B.   The area immediately outside of the apartment where the Respondents were guests qualifies as curtilage because there can be a reasonable expectation of privacy despite lack of property rights in the building or land in question.

    C.   It should have been evident to the police officer making the observations that he was intruding into the privacy of the home because of the circumstances under which he made the observations.

Here is one attempt at a revision. Note how the revised set of headings uses more specifics ("Officer Thielen," "Thompson's apartment") and are shorter than the originals. To make the point about length more emphatic, you might block and copy the headings so that each revision is directly below the original.

II. Officer Thielen conducted a search when he stood inches from Thompson's building and looked through the window because he stood within the residence's curtilage.

    A. Officer Thielen invaded the curtilage of Thompson's apartment when he left the normal walkway and positioned himself within eighteen inches of her window.

    B. Both curtilage and a reasonable expectation of privacy can exist even without property rights in a building or its surrounding land.

    C. Officer Thielen should have known that he was intruding into the privacy of a home because of the circumstances of his observation.

Other Ideas for Group Exercises/Demonstrations:

1. Write persuasive question(s) presented for the respondent in <u>Miller v. Albright</u>.

2. Read a statement of the case from the appendix (or from a teacher handout) and identify where the writer used a) the buddy system, b) juxtaposition or pointillism, c) details v. more abstract language, d) narrative reasoning or storytelling techniques and/or e) other persuasive techniques.

3. **Before class,** have students send you via e-mail excerpts from one or all of the special team items in which they tried a persuasive technique. They should explain what they were trying to accomplish and how they used the technique to accomplish the goal.

4. If there is a particularly difficult fact that each side has to deal with, break the students into groups and have both sides write about it (even better if there's a fact that's bad for each and you can have each group write about its own bad fact and the other side's bad fact). Have the groups share their paragraphs, and discuss how each side handled the good or bad fact.

5. Have students turn in a set of point headings; pull good and classic bad examples and discuss common problems.

Significant New Vocabulary:
    Enthymemes
    Juxtaposition
    Pointillism
    Schemas
    Stock stories

Chapter Ten
Six Degrees of Legal Writing: Making Your Document Reader-Friendly

Possible Teaser(s) for Syllabus:

    What is Oprah Winfrey's real "Bacon Number"? (Section 10.1)

    What does Kevin Bacon have to do with legal writing? (Section 10.1)

    What is your issue's backstory? (Section 10.2.3)

Learning Goals of Class Meeting:

This class has two related goals:

Teaching students the "Kevin Bacon" metaphor to encourage them to articulate how each part of the argument connects to the overall thesis of the brief (or to another significant part of the argument)

Teaching them how to create and use "template items" to allow their readers to find and use the various pieces of their arguments more easily.

Changes from Second Edition:

This chapter expands the discussion of Topic Sentences to focus on how to use topic sentences in the explanation section as a method to lay a foundation for analogizing or distinguishing authority cases. The "roadmap" section of the chapter introduces the concept of "legal backstory" to describe the information that should appear in introductory material that precedes the roadmap.

Audio-visual aids on Website:

The Website includes a powerpoint on the template.

The Website also includes a powerpoint on using effective topic sentences in the explanation section (i.e., combining topic sentences and case descriptions). (I usually use this later in the semester to review the lessons of this chapter combined with the lessons of chapter 6)

Possible pre-class assignments in addition to the reading:

Have students e-mail you a "Kevin Bacon string" by choosing an actor from a movie that has some connection to the issue that the case presents. E.g., for a medical marijuana case, I had the students "Kevin Bacon" Brenda Blethyn, who starred in "Saving Grace," a movie about a woman who grows marijuana. When students wrote about a male coach of a woman's team who sued for sex discrimination, I had them "Kevin Bacon" Parminder Nagra, who starred in "Bend it Like Beckham," a movie about a woman who plays soccer against her parents' wishes on a team coached by a man. I could have had students "Kevin Bacon" Tom Hanks, who starred in "A League of Their Own," about a women's baseball team coached by a man. Since Tom Hanks was in a famous movie with Kevin Bacon ("Apollo 13"), I thought that was too easy. Some students who do the reading will use the "Oracle of Bacon at Virginia" to complete the assignment, which means their "chain" of Bacon links will be short. You may wish to make one that is a little longer to illustrate the point of the exercise.

If and when you review the lessons of chapter 6 combined with the lessons of this chapter, you might ask students to e-mail you or bring a copy of a case description of a particular case. A perfect case to assign would be a case that is significant to each side's argument (although they may differ about its relevance). In the alternative, you could ask petitioners and respondents to bring separate case descriptions. If I have the students bring the assignment to class, I will accept it if they have a copy of their current draft of the brief that contains a description of the case.

Ideas for Teaching/Discussion:

Kevin Bacon

Although the Kevin Bacon idea is new (the game may be new to some of the students, which is why the text explains it), most students easily get the concept of connecting ideas within their arguments to each other and/or to their main thesis. As with many ideas about writing, the execution of the idea is more difficult than understanding it. Although it would not be unreasonable to ask students to create "Kevin Bacon links" to a sample document, it is an idea that is hard to do in isolation. Thus, in class I spend time explaining the game and the idea and going through a couple of illustrations of the idea (from the examples in the text and by calling on students to give me their links). The reinforcement comes mostly in my critiques of their work, when I ask them to "Kevin Bacon" an idea to their overall thesis or to a related section, or when I compliment them on having provided needed "Bacon links." (Yes, that *is* a horrible pun on sausage links.) For example, in a recent statutory interpretation case that my students worked on, many of them simply started talking about legislative history without providing the needed "Bacon links" to explain how it fit into their argument (i.e., that it's all right to go to legislative history when the language of the statute is ambiguous, and that their language was ambiguous, so . . . .).

The better that the writer understands the argument as a whole and as its component parts, the better the writer will be able to provide the needed Bacon links. One idea for reinforcing the concept would be to ask the students to tell you *some* point that they would be making in their briefs, and then ask them to Kevin Bacon that point to their main thesis of affirming or reversing the Court below. In the alternative, *you* could tell *them* some point from one of the sample briefs and ask them to Kevin Bacon that point, using the brief if the brief provides the links, or pointing out that the brief does not provide the links.

For example, in section II.B.2. of the petitioner's brief in <u>Minnesota v. Carter</u>, the writer makes the point that Officer Thielen "made no physical intrusion and used no device to enhance his natural senses." To Kevin Bacon that point:

Because Officer Thielen made no physical intrusion and used only his natural senses, he did not use extraordinary measures.

Because he did not use extraordinary measures, he did not violate a reasonable expectation of privacy.

Because he did not violate a reasonable expectation of privacy, he did not conduct a fourth amendment search.

Because he did not conduct a fourth amendment search, this Court must reverse.

(Some students might want to add another link -- that the Court below erred when it found that a fourth amendment search did occur.) Once the students have identified the links, ask them where in the brief (if anywhere) they found the links. These links can be found at the end of section II.B.2. They can also be pieced together from the introductory material at the beginning of Section II.B.2, Section II.B., and Section II. Because some students feel that they are being "too obvious" if they make their connections so explicit, you might want to emphasize how explicit connections help the reader to find and comprehend the writer's points. The discussion about "installing a template" is a good place to talk about Bacon links, because most of the Bacon links appear in template items (i.e., roadmaps and connection-conclusions).

Installing a Template

Two of the template items should be familiar to the students already: headings and connection-conclusions. Many students will also be familiar with the concepts of topic sentences and roadmap paragraphs. The text contains examples of how these items can be used effectively in legal writing, and none of them are very difficult individually.

I teach this chapter in the order in which I would *write* these template items on a desperation brief. I sometimes talk about the future, about the times when they won't have ten weeks to write a brief. Sometimes they will simply have to get the brief out the door on a very short deadline. In those situations, when they may have time to do little more than write a "dump draft," the best thing they can do for their reader is to organize the document and provide signals to that organization with the template items. Thus, writing the topic sentences can tell you how to organize the whole argument and can identify places where you need headings. The headings, in turn, can signal where you need internal roadmap paragraphs and connection-conclusions.

To make sure the students understand the importance of topic sentences, try to get the students to admit that they sometimes skip paragraphs if the topic sentence doesn't make the paragraph seem worthwhile. The book makes this point, but it is talking about some vague, unknown reader. If they realize that they themselves engage in certain behavior, they may be more likely to write in a way that takes this behavior into account. I freely admit to my students that I have skipped paragraphs when doing functional reading (not when critiquing their papers, of course).

The formula for topic sentences is focused on the explanation section, but at least one aspect -- the phrase-that-pays -- may be useful in all topic sentences. The students may have other ideas, such as picking up other key terms or ideas from the brief. You may wish to find a "real" brief and ask the students to evaluate the effectiveness of the topic sentences, or ask them to evaluate the effectiveness of the topic sentences in one or more of the sample briefs. To the extent that they think certain sentences are less effective, how would they revise? The example in Section 10.2.1 of the text shows how topic sentences can be revised to incorporate a phrase-that-pays.

Further, the topic sentence powerpoint shows examples of how topic sentences can be used effectively in the explanation section. If and when you focus on topic sentences and rule explanation, have the petitioners sit on one side of the room and the respondents on the other. You can ask them to write up an effective case description for the assigned case. They can e-mail you their responses (if you have a wired classroom) or pass them to the front to be reviewed on a document camera. Then, have them write an effective topic sentence for that paragraph, one that focuses on what the case tells the reader about the phrase-that-pays.

When addressing this chapter, I usually do not spend much time, if any, on the concepts of either headings and connection-conclusions, other than to discuss the need for them and soliciting student questions.

Roadmap paragraphs will be a new concept for some students, but most should have learned something about them in an earlier legal writing course (perhaps under a different name, such as "thesis paragraphs" or "umbrella section"). What might be a new concept is the concept of "legal backstory" as well as the need for internal roadmaps in a complex document. If you wanted to give the class practice in drafting effective roadmap paragraphs, you could copy one of the sample briefs from the back of the text, remove the internal roadmaps, and reassemble the document. Ask the students to close their textbooks and then distribute your "unroadmapped" version. Ask the students to draft introductions and/or roadmap paragraphs as needed, and then compare them to the final version, in Appendix C. Sometimes your students will do a better job.

You might also ask your students to work in pairs to write up the legal backstory to their case. You might want to lead a discussion on how much information the reader needs to know, how much detail is appropriate, etc.

Significant vocabulary for Chapter Ten:

Legal backstory
Template items
Six Degrees of Kevin Bacon

Chapter Eleven
Exploiting Opportunities for Persuasion

Possible Teaser(s) for Syllabus:

How does *Scrabble* relate to legal writing? (Section 11.1)
Be ready to distinguish between positive and negative intensifiers (Section 11.4.5)
What is the "gigolo" of the punctuation world, and who called it that? (Section 11.4.6(b))

Learning Goals of Class Meeting:

To discuss the possibilities and limitations of persuasive writing techniques
To understand their impact and how to accomplish them

Changes from Second Edition:

No major changes.

Aids on the website:

The website contains a powerpoint that you can use to illustrate many of the points. I think it contains a particularly good illustration of the power of active v. passive voice (that is also described below).

Possible pre-class assignments beyond the readings:

You could ask your students to review their work to identify a place in which their writing illustrates one of the concepts mentioned in the chapter (e.g., use of active or passive voice by design, use of colon for emphasis, etc.). They can find an example or write or revise something using persuasive techniques, and send it with an explanation of what they're trying to accomplish with the technique (or what the technique accomplishes, if they did it unconsciously).

Ideas for Lecture and Discussion:

Although this topic can certainly fit in with other chapters, you may use this chapter to discuss the significance of reputation to attorney credibility. Most of our students have no history but school, where work is often submitted and judged anonymously. Thus, they have little comprehension of the impact of reputation. If you have war stories from practice about the knowledge of your firm's reputation, or the reputation of attorneys or firms who opposed your firm, this might be a good time to discuss it (you need not name names!). You might even ask your students who have worked in law firms if they were aware of the reputations of any of their opponents.

Related to reputation is the concept of the limits of persuasive writing techniques. Attorneys have the job of explaining the law and the facts to the Court. If at least one side provides this information with a certain degree of accuracy, the law will dictate the result of more than half of the cases. This chapter is written for those cases in which advocacy or writing techniques may tip the balance. Attorneys must use these techniques honestly in all cases, however, so that they have a reservoir of credibility and reliable advocacy that can be drawn upon when needed.

The text contains examples of nearly every type of persuasive writing technique. You may want to reproduce these on overheads to have available if questions arise, or you may want to develop your own examples, or have your students develop their own examples, to illustrate their points.

Because most of the concepts are not intellectually challenging, I do not spend too much time addressing how the various techniques work. The main exception to this guideline is the concept of active and passive voice. I find that the rules about passive voice are not unlike the infield fly rule -- easily learned, and easily forgotten. Thus, if I have time, I will spend some time in class with students on how active and passive voice work and why they make a difference in legal writing.

The text does not include my favorite illustration of the impact of active v. passive voice because it has more impact in class than in a text; it is below, and in the powerpoint on the website. I ask the students if they have ever received a rejection letter, and then I show them an actual sentence from a rejection letter I once received:

In the end, we decided that other people are better qualified than you.

Many students, properly, will gasp at the rudeness of the sentence; I sometimes give myself a mock slap in the face to illustrate the point. Then I ask why the sentence is so rude. I get a lot of responses along the lines of "it's so direct." Only rarely will a student make the connection and say "it's in active voice." If they don't, I will point this out, which often leads a student to protest, "but I thought active voice was better!" I note that I am not there to make value judgments; both active and passive voice have their places; active voice is simply more *direct*. More direct is usually better, but not always. During this discussion, I also show a more common rejection-letter sentence:

In the end, a decision was made that preferable qualifications are possessed by others.

I ask the students to explain why this letter is less rude. Someone may point out the obvious that it is less direct, and we talk about how it will take the reader a while to realize, "hey . . . I don't think they like me here . . . . ." The sentence also has no actor; the reader has to deduce who made the decision. This sentence can transition to a discussion of nominalizations, for the active voice verb phrase "we decided" was transformed into the passive nominalization "a decision was made."

A couple of different in-class exercises suggest themselves. First is just the ability to identify passive voice verbs. You may wish to put an excerpt of text onto the overhead and ask students to identify the verbs (that alone will be a challenge for some) and then label the verbs as either active or passive. The example below is printed twice; once blank, for use on an overhead, and once with <u>active voice verbs underlined</u> and **passive voice verbs in bold-faced type**. (It is also part of the powerpoint.) This example is adapted from a fact statement in a student-respondent's brief in the case of <u>Holloway v. United States</u>:

> The Petitioner's involvement in this crime ring began in September of 1994 when he was invited by his lifelong friend, Vernon Lennon, to carjack cars for Lennon's father, Teddy Arnold. R. 355. Arnold owned a "chop shop" in Queens that was responsible for dismantling many stolen cars each day. R. 312. Lennon would receive a request from Arnold for a certain year and type of car. R. 356. The car would be stolen later that same day, and then would be delivered to Arnold's chop shop in Queens. R. 357.
>
> During the carjackings, Lennon and the Petitioner, implicitly or explicitly, threatened these victims to either give up their cars or die. R. 359. Lennon never shot his victims – who were terrified by his threats – because he knew that a shooting would subject him to a longer prison sentence. R. 342. Nonetheless, he did state that he would have shot the victims "if their resistance made that necessary." R. 343. In other words, he intended to kill or seriously injure the victims, but that intent was dependent on whether the victims gave the robbers "a hard time." R. 344.

> The Petitioner's involvement in this crime ring <u>began</u> in September of 1994 when he **was invited** by his lifelong friend, Vernon Lennon, <u>to carjack</u> cars for Lennon's father, Teddy Arnold. R. 355. Arnold <u>owned</u> a "chop shop" in Queens that <u>was</u> responsible for dismantling many stolen cars each day. R. 312. Lennon would <u>receive</u> a request from Arnold for a certain year and type of car. R. 356. The car would **be stolen** later that same day, and then would **be delivered** to Arnold's chop shop in Queens. R. 357.
>
> During the carjackings, Lennon and the Petitioner, implicitly or explicitly, <u>threatened</u> these victims to either give up their cars or die. R. 359. Lennon never <u>shot</u> his victims – who **were terrified** by his threats – because he <u>knew</u> that a shooting would <u>subject</u> him to a longer prison sentence. R. 342. Nonetheless, he did <u>state</u> that he would have <u>shot</u> the victims "if their resistance <u>made</u> that necessary." R. 343. In other words, he <u>intended</u> to kill or seriously injure the victims, but that intent <u>was</u> dependent on whether the victims <u>gave</u> the robbers "a hard time." R. 344.

In addition to noting which verbs are in active or passive voice, you might ask the students whether the writer made a good choice; would it be more or less persuasive if written the other way? If you really want to reinforce the skill, you could ask the students to revise the paragraphs, changing all active voice verbs to passive voice verbs, and all passive voice verbs to active voice verbs. They may revise other parts of the sentence if necessary to achieve the goal. Their result might look something like this example, which succeeds in changing most of the verbs:

> In September of 1994 the Petitioner's involvement in this crime ring was begun

[by petitioner]. His lifelong friend, Vernon Lennon, invited him and told him that cars had to be carjacked by him for Lennon's father, Teddy Arnold. R. 355. A "chop shop" in Queens was owned by Arnold; many stolen cars were dismantled there each day. R. 312. A request from Arnold would be received by Lennon for a certain year and type of car. R. 356. Lennon and the Petitioner would steal the car later that same day, and then he would deliver it to Arnold's chop shop in Queens. R. 357.

During the carjackings, the victims were threatened by Lennon and the Petitioner, implicitly or explicitly, that their cars must be given up or their death would be experienced. R. 359. The victims were never shot by Lennon – although his threats terrified them – because it was known by Lennon that he would be subjected to a longer prison sentence if they were shot by him. R. 342. Nonetheless, it was stated by Lennon that his victims would have been shot by him "if their resistance made that necessary." R. 343. In other words, it was intended by Lennon that the victims would be killed or seriously injured by him, but that intent was dependent on whether the robbers were given "a hard time" by the victims. R. 344.

In the alternative, you could ask the students to study a brief from the appendix or from a case you designated and try to identify as many persuasive writing techniques as possible.

If you want to conduct in-class work, you could ask the petitioners and the respondents to gather in groups and brainstorm about what significant points they might make, and to write a sentence or paragraph using one or more of the persuasive techniques in the chapter. For example, you could ask one group to write a sentence using a colon, another to write a short sentence, another to use the dash to highlight a piece of information, another to write a passive voice sentence to de-emphasize information, etc. You might ask one group to write sentences that make points that should be in positions of emphasis in the brief -- in other words, ask the students to articulate their most significant points.

Significant vocabulary for Chapter Eleven:

Nominalizations
Psycholinguistics
Positions of Emphasis
Active and Passive voice
Justification
Document Design

Chapter Twelve
Polishing

Possible Teaser for Syllabus:

We will discuss how your computer can help (Sec. 12.1) and hurt (12.3) your ability to proofread your document.

Learning Goals for Class:s

Importance of proofreading
Using a variety of methods

Changes from Second Edition:

Nothing significant; the chapter includes another method for easing proofreading on the computer: Enlarging text to a larger font. Teachers should be sure that students understand that this method is to use only when proofreading and that font must be returned to normal size before filing the document. (!)

Possible pre-class assignments in addition to the reading:

I send my students an e-mail the morning of class, with the header "do not open until instructed during class." It contains a version of the "Amtrak unit of discourse" seeded with proofreading mistakes.

Aids on the Website

The website contains the mistake-seeded version of the Amtrak unit of discourse, and another version with the mistakes marked. The powerpoint combines elements from chapter 11 and chapter 12. Your course timing may make it appropriate to spread this powerpoint over two classes, or to divide it in other ways.

Ideas for Class Discussion:

Again, because most of the ideas in this chapter are self-evident, this chapter does not need much illustration. You may want to tell war stories about the importance of proofreading. (As noted above, a good source might be Judith D. Fischer, *Bareheaded and Barefaced Counsel: Courts React to Unprofessionalism in Lawyers' Papers*, 31 Suffolk Univ. L. Rev. 1 (1997)). Depending on the personality of your class, you might be able to engage them in a discussion about the various proofreading methods that they use when doing their own work. Ideally, they will feel comfortable sharing such ideas, and they can learn from each other.

If you have discovered that certain types of errors dominate their earlier drafts, you may want to devote some class time to addressing these errors. For example, if citation form errors are a problem, you may want to devote time to a quick review of citation form problems. Because the proofreading class is usually my last class of the semester, you may want to make it like the review session of an exam-based class, and allow students to bring any questions they may have to you OR, in the alternative, to e-mail those questions to you in advance so you can answer them publicly without revealing who asked what. Let them know that if the class ends early, you will remain to answer questions privately, *but that they shouldn't count on there being time for you to get to every person's private question.* This warning may encourage the shy ones to ask you in advance, particularly if you create an in-box on the front table for students to put their questions in (anonymously) before class begins.

You may use the proofreading exercise or make up one of your own designed to hit the problems your students encounter most commonly. If you use the exercise, bring hard copies for people who don't have laptop access. It may be interesting to note if the laptop proofreaders find errors differently than the hard copy proofreaders; that may lead to a discussion of doing both kinds of proofreading.

Chapter Thirteen
Oral Argument

Possible Teaser for Syllabus:

In class, we will discuss "getting through your stuff." (Section 13.6)
Be ready to explain why oral argument is not like a quiz show. (Section 13.6)

Learning Goals for Class Session:

Teach students how to prepare for an effective oral argument
Calm students' fears about oral argument.

Changes from Second Edition:

Chapter 13 now gives advice on keeping a poker face when arguing, and gives more specific advice on what to do when asked a question that you don't understand.

Possible pre-class assignments beyond the reading:

Students are usually so nervous about oral argument that they read this chapter intently. If you want to promote preparation, you may wish to ask them to prepare an oral argument outline.

Aids on the website:

The website contains a powerpoint presentation on oral argument.

Ideas for Class Discussion:

The website that accompanies this Teacher's Manual contains a power point presentation that you can use or adapt for your class. If you choose the "View" toolbar, and the "Notes Page," entry, you can print out the slides with notes about ways to use each slide in class. If you wish to read or alter the notes before you print them, go to the "View" toolbar, and choose the "Slide" entry. This should bring up the slides individually. Then, go back to the "View" toolbar and choose the "Speaker notes" entry. This will show the speaker notes in a separate box on top of each slide (although you can use your mouse to move the speaker notes over to one side or the other). Some slides are self-explanatory and have no notes.

Instead of or in addition to the power point presentation, however, you may decide to use other teaching techniques. Your students will probably be very nervous, and thus very attentive. I always have a list of points to talk about, but at times I have let students direct the class, going in and asking them, "what do you want to talk about, about oral argument?" or "what are you worried about when you think about oral argument?" I write these items on the board, trying to place them in the order in which I'd like to talk about them, and then I use the students' questions as an outline for my lecture and as a springboard for discussion.

If you are very comfortable talking about oral argument *and* have the right climate in your classroom, you might present part of your lecture as an oral argument. You would be the advocate, and the students would all be the judges. If your class is a large one, you could exercise control over things by designating a panel of several students, and then asking the rest to funnel their questions through those students. I have never tried this method before, but I think it could be very effective in a small class, or in a large one with a designated panel.

Of course, you should put a time limit on the oral argument so that you can lead a discussion about what occurred, e.g., "did you notice that I was quiet when I was asked questions?" "Did I answer all of the questions directly?" etc. Further, if your class is a small one, you might try some method that would allow or require each student to speak. Some of my adjuncts have told me about using this method, which may have originated in NITA training sessions. Make a list of random statements relevant to popular culture and put them in a box. Make each student draw out a statement, read it aloud, and instantly present an argument defending the point. For example, "The Daily Show is better than the Colbert Report," "the minimum age for driver's licenses should be 18," "green is a better color than orange," etc. Even though they will not be interrupted by questions (unless you do it yourself or require students to do it), most students will appreciate getting their feet wet with a short oral presentation.

Because oral argument transcripts are available on Lexis and Westlaw, and transcripts from the 2000 term onward are available on the U.S. Supreme Court website (http://www.supremecourtus.gov/oral_arguments/argument_transcripts.html), you might want to look up an interesting transcript and use it as the basis for part of your class discussion. For example, I have sometimes recruited students to do a "dramatic reading" from the oral argument in Bentsen v. Coors.

There are several things to note about this excerpt, which is from the end of the respondent's argument. First, I explain to the class that Coors had been accused of bringing the cause of action – which would allow them to put the percentage of alcohol in its beer onto the label -- only because they were tired of being known as a weak beer ("Colorado Kool-Aid"). Some of the attorney's answers try to show that this justification, even if accurate, is not the only reason behind the lawsuit. Students will also note how the attorney had specific knowledge about the facts behind the case – he knew about his client's business, the manufacturing of beer. He was not afraid to contradict the justices when they were wrong, and he also used his answers to bring the justices back to his theme (his theme was getting accurate alcohol content info to beer-drinker, or, to use the attorney's word choice, getting truthful information to consumers). See if the students can recognize the friendly "question," when one of the judges says, "but we can't know any of this from the label." The excerpt begins with a question from Justice Scalia:

Justice One: What is ale? What's the difference between ale and beer?

Mr. Ennis: Well, to the best of my knowledge, Justice Scalia, ale is a malt beverage, but it is produced quite differently from beer. Beer is what's called a bottom fermentation process, and ale is a top fermentation process.

Justice One: Ah, that explains it. (Laughter.)

162

Mr. Ennis: Well, I guess it's something--I guess--I'm not sure, but I think it's something like milk in the old days before it was homogenized. The cream on the top of the milk would be the equivalent of the ale, and the rest of the milk would be the equivalent of the beer.

Justice One: Which is malt liquor, top or bottom?

Mr. Ennis: Pardon?

Justice One: Is malt liquor top or bottom?

Mr. Ennis: Well, malt liquor is the highest strength--

Justice One: I know it's the highest strength, but--

Mr. Ennis:--malt beverage.

Justice Two: Is that the only difference between it and--ale and beer, that it's got more alcohol in it?

Mr. Ennis: No. There is another difference, Your Honor, which is the reason why most consumers don't--only 3 percent, historically, of consumers choose malt liquor. The other difference is, as you increase the alcohol strength, you necessarily increase the bitterness, the harshness, the roughness of the taste, and therefore malt liquor has a much rougher, harsher taste than lower alcohol products, which is precisely why most producers are targeting the mid-market and lower. Coors, for example, two-thirds of Coors' sales are of its light beer product, which is 4.1 percent alcohol. That's what they asked permission to do, to say that our light beer is 4.1 percent alcohol. Clearly, Coors was not trying to attract the high strength market there, because 4.1 percent is at the low end, the bottom end of the mainstream range of beers in this country, and why would Coors, which gets two-thirds of its revenue from selling a light beer, want to abandon that market, increase the beer strength, lose those customers, and compete for 3 percent of the market?

Justice Three: Well, light beer doesn't mean--has nothing to do with alcoholic content.

Mr. Ennis: It does have a great deal to do with alcohol content, Chief Justice Rehnquist. It's not one-to-one, but there is a one-to-one correlation between calories and alcohol, and light beer is supposed to be lower in calories, as it is, and in order to do that, it's necessary to make it lower in alcohol content as well.

Justice Two: So your typical light beer will have less alcohol content?

Mr. Ennis: Your typical light beer will have less alcohol content. There is a range

Chapter Thirteen

of alcohol contents in light beers, however, and that's what Coors wanted consumers to know. They wanted–

Justice Three: But is it a fact that in the Tenth Circuit argument Coors disclosed that its reason for this litigation was to dispel the notion that Coors is a weak beer?

Mr. Ennis: Your Honor--

Justice Three: Was that part of the argument?

Mr. Ennis: I was not there, but that's apparently what the transcript reflects, Your Honor. Coors did want to dispel misleading impressions about the strength of its products, but what it wanted to disclose was the accurate, honest information about the strength of its products, and that information would have shown that its products were not the high strength products. The Coors light beer is 4.1 percent-- that's what it wanted to say--which is at the low end. The other product it wanted permission to label was its regular beer, which is 4.6 percent, which is the very mid-point of the range in this country. It's not a high strength product at all. Coors was obviously not trying to market its product to attract the high strength--

Justice Two: 4.1 is the low end of beers, but not the low end of lights, I gather.

Mr. Ennis: I think it's probably about in the middle of lights, Your Honor.

Justice One: But we can't know any of this by looking at the label. (Laughter.)

Mr. Ennis: You can't. You can't. You cannot. If you happen to be in one of the two-thirds of the States of this country that permit advertising, you can learn that from the advertising, including advertising right in the beer store next to the label, but this Federal law bans that information from the label itself. It obviously cannot directly and materially advance the Federal Government's interests because of that fact, and even if it did, as I pointed out earlier, there is a simple, more effective way to control the strength war problem the Government currently asserts simply by limiting the alcohol content except in States that permit a higher limit. The Government has conceded that that would achieve--fully achieve its strength wars interest. There's no reason to ban truthful, accurate, and important information in these circumstances. Thank you very much.

Justice Three: Thank you, Mr. Ennis. Mr. Kneedler, you have 2 minutes remaining.

Furthermore, you may wish to let students listen to oral argument excerpts and hear how the give and take occurs. A Northwestern University website (http://oyez.org), familiarly known as The Oyez Site, has audio access to the oral arguments in many cases, including Bush v. Gore. You may wish to **spend some time before class reviewing oral arguments** and finding good excerpts to cue up during your class time. Due to the vagaries of the web, I always recommend having a backup plan ready in case access is denied. You may wish to purchase the CD-ROM, "The

Supreme Court's Greatest Hits," which is listed for purchase on The Oyez Site. The CD-ROM may allow more specific searching of the oral argument, and gives other information about the cases as well. Recognize that both on the site and on the CD-ROM, quality of the audio varies wildly, depending on what happened at the time of recording.

If you have the time and the ability, you may try to listen to this excerpt from Vernonia School District v. Acton. The audio is available on the Oyez Site, and while the sound quality is not perfect, one excerpt of the argument is worth listening to. (http://www.oyez.org/cases/1990-1999/1994/1994_94_590) Invariably, I end up telling the students what to listen for. It is sometimes worth it -- the shout of laughter in the courtroom is quite amazing. The issue in that case was the ability of a school district to perform suspicionless drug testing of its high school athletes. One of the justices, I believe Justice Breyer, was trying to get at just how "private" the act of urination is. Counsel for the student, Mr. Christ, revealed his nervousness and stopped the show:

> QUESTION: All right. Well then, the problem, of course, for people is, if they can require the physical exams for the health, and I guess you could require medical-- metal detectors to keep guns out of schools, a lot of things you can require, what's different about this?

> MR. CHRIST: Because this is so highly intrusive.

> QUESTION: Medical exams all involve urinalyses.

> MR. CHRIST: That's–

> QUESTION: I've probably had hundreds of them in my life, and so have you, and you know, what's the special thing here?

> MR. CHRIST: The medical exam you're talking about is being conducted in private by the student's doctor. It is not being conducted–

> QUESTION: Well, people urinate, you know, in men's rooms all over the country. It's not necessarily--and I don't mean to be--trivialize it, but it isn't really a tremendously private thing, is it?
> MR. CHRIST: I think it is private when it is being compelled by the Government, and the Government is there watching and observing and collecting specimens.

> QUESTION: All right. What I'm trying to get you to do is to pinpoint precisely what it is that's the intrusion of the privacy interest. That's what I'm trying–

> MR. CHRIST: It's not–

> QUESTION: That's what I'm aiming at.

> MR. CHRIST: It's not the mere act. We all urinate. That's--has to be conceded. (Laughter.)

MR. CHRIST: In fact, I might do so here. . . (Laughter.)

Chapter Fourteen
Moot Court Competitions

Possible Teasers for Syllabus:
   What "unique insight" does this chapter contain? (Section 14.6)

Teaching Goals for the Class:
   I don't assign this chapter to my students in the basic appellate advocacy course, but I may recommend that they review Section 14.5; sometimes students will be more likely to read an assignment that they think will give them a "hidden benefit."

Changes from Second Edition:

No significant changes.

Possible pre-class assignments in addition to the readings:

N/A

Audio-Visual Aids

N/A

Ideas for Discussion/Group Work:
   If you are coaching a Moot Court team, you may want to ask them to read this chapter before you meet with them so that you can flush out questions they may have about how the competition will work. Go through the rule book with them and establish any due dates for drafts or dates for meetings. If appropriate, talk with them about how they will divide up the work.

   Presuming that your team does not have a long winning streak at the relevant competition (in which case you would not deign to read advice from another anyway), look at the winning briefs from previous years and compare them with the briefs submitted by your schools. With your practiced eye, compare the winning and "losing" brief and look for patterns, such as use of authority, perfection in small things, clear organization, etc. Editing another's brief is much easier than editing your own, but if you are a coach who can't help on the brief-writing process, you can teach brief-writing skills by looking at briefs from past years and pointing out common problems and important things that the winning briefs did right.

   Many competitions videotape the final round of the competition and make that tape available for purchase. Viewing this videotape can be soothing in some ways, for most students will see techniques that they are capable of reproducing. I recommend watching the tape before they start working on the brief, or while they are still in the early stages. Even if they feel that the performance of the winning teams is beyond their abilities, you will probably recognize that it is not significantly different from the performances of teams you have coached in past years, and thus, that this team has the potential to develop their skills to that level. In many competitions, however, the brief score has to be high in order for even a team with the strongest oral skills to advance in the competition. Thus, viewing the oral argument tape can encourage the team to work harder on their brief.

Significant vocabulary for Chapter Fourteen:
Cold courts and hot courts